The Giant with One Idea

D1381490

The Giant with One Idea

Thomas Clarkson

Emily J. Maurits

CF4·K

10 9 8 7 6 5 4 3 2 1

Copyright © 2021 Emily J. Maurits
Paperback ISBN: 978-1-5271-0677-2
epub ISBN: 978-1-5271-0751-9
mobi ISBN: 978-1-5271-0752-6

Published by Christian Focus Publications,
Geanies House, Fearn, Tain, Ross-shire,
IV20 1TW, Scotland, U.K.
www.christianfocus.com;
email: info@christianfocus.com

Cover design by Daniel van Straaten
Cover illustration by Jeff Anderson
Printed and bound by Nørhaven, Denmark

Contents

To Amelia
Josh &
Sherwin
– Thank you.

In his Father's Footsteps

'Why isn't Father home yet?' Six-year-old Thomas Clarkson stared out the window at the shadowy street.

'He's out visiting,' his older sister Anne said, settling herself into the chair beside him. 'Do you know about the awful sickness spreading through the parish?'

Thomas nodded, pulling his hands away from the cold pane of glass. As well as the curate of the adjoining parish, Father was headmaster of Wisbech Free Grammar School, and Thomas had heard him mention that several students had been ill recently and unable to attend class.

'But it looks so frightening out there,' he said. 'Why does he have to visit the sick families now?'

Anne laughed. 'When else is he going to visit them? He teaches during the day, so must visit at night. There aren't enough hours in the day to fit in everything Father wants to do!'

'And there never will be, bless him.' Thomas' mother swept into the room, carrying baby John on her hip. 'Time for bed, Thomas.' She reached over and ruffled Thomas' red hair. Twenty-five years younger than her husband, Thomas' mother was well known for her good looks, and was more than capable of keeping pace with her energetic husband.

'I want to wait up until Father gets home,' Thomas protested. 'What if he gets lost?'

His mother smiled. 'Tom, what is it that your father always takes with him when he goes out visiting?'

'His big lantern.'

'Exactly.' Mrs. Clarkson held out a hand to her oldest son. 'With that huge contraption to light up his way, he can't help but get back to town safely.'

Thomas remembered the bright light Father's heavy metal lamp emitted. His mother was right. Still ... 'Maybe I could just wait up a little longer?'

Anne laughed. 'A little longer won't help! Father's not likely to be finished until midnight at least.'

Mother nodded, though she pulled John closer to her side and cast a glance out the window, just as Thomas had done. They could all hear the clap-clap of loose doors and roof tiles as the wind whipped through the street below. It really was very stormy tonight! Thomas hoped no one had left a window open in the school room beneath them. The draught would surely tear across the desks, scattering papers and ink pots everywhere.

'Perhaps I should check to see if the school is alright.'

'Perhaps, my stubborn Thomas,' his mother said, turning back to him, 'you should go to bed as I told you to.'

Out of excuses, Thomas followed Mother into his bedroom. As she tucked him in, he had one last question. 'But what does Father do?' he asked. 'He's a clergyman and teacher – not a doctor!' Thomas paused. 'Or is he?'

'No,' Mother smiled. 'Two occupations are quite enough! You know how we had a nice hot supper tonight, and now you're tucked up in a warm bed, even though it's very cold outside?'

Thomas nodded.

'Well,' continued his mother, 'not everyone has a hot supper and a warm bed. There are some poor people in the parish who don't have either of those things, and they don't have the money for medicine when they get ill. Your father tries to help by bringing them what they need. He also tells them the good news of the Bible, that Jesus cares about all people, even if they are poor and sick.'

Thomas, eyes half-closed, was almost asleep. Already the sounds of the storm seemed very far away. As his mother blew out the candle beside his bed, he had one last question. 'Do all clergymen care about the poor like Father does?'

Mother paused. 'Not all.'

'Why not?'

Thomas' mother sighed. 'Sometimes helping other people is hard work and uncomfortable. It's easier to turn away and pretend you haven't seen. But your father knows that if you love God you cannot ignore those in trouble.'

***

Bang!

Thomas woke with a jerk. His bedroom was dark, and he wondered why he had woken. It was still the middle of the night. The wind howled against the window. Then Thomas heard his father's voice, and his mother answering. Burrowing deeper into his blankets, he smiled as he closed his eyes again.

Father was home.

***

A few days later, Thomas watched as the men lowered his father's casket into the ground. Around him people cried and sobbed. The churchyard was crowded with all the families his father had helped and all the students he had taught. Many shops and businesses in town had boarded up their doors to attend the funeral.

His father had been greatly loved.

As the church bell tolled a low, plaintive call, Thomas rubbed his eyes, still unable to believe what was happening. His father had caught the fever while visiting, and before anything could be done, the God he had served so faithfully had called him home.

After the funeral, Thomas' mother tried to smile at her children. 'It's going to be alright,' she said. 'My cousin has given us a house on High Street, so we won't have to move far. It will be an adventure.'

'Can we take Father's lamp?' Thomas wanted to know. The heavy metal lantern was the strongest connection he had to his father now. He didn't like to think of them leaving it behind for the next schoolmaster.

'Of course!' Mother said. 'We will keep it always.'

***

'Will you miss this?' Nine years later, eleven-year-old John Clarkson waved a hand to include the wide, grey River Nene at their feet, the town of Wisbech immediately behind them, and the marshy fens stretching out to the horizon.

'Of course.' To most people, Wisbech wasn't a particularly pretty part of Cambridgeshire, and Thomas had to admit he always enjoyed the months they spent in Essex visiting their cousins. Still, Wisbech had always been home, and Thomas thought there was something beautiful in the flat fields laced with ditches and low walls. 'But if I want to be a clergyman like Father, I have to go to London to study.'

John snorted. 'You can keep your books. I'm going to sea,' he said, kicking at a loose cobble as he gazed at the ships swaying in Wisbech Port. 'I'll have adventures and fight off pirates and defend England!'

Thomas laughed. It sounded like the perfect occupation for his enthusiastic younger brother. At fifteen years old, Thomas had to admit that adventures on the sea did sound exciting. 'But I can't wait to see London,' he said, focussing on his own adventure.

John was still studying the tall ships' masts. 'Do you want to be a teacher too, like Father?'

'No.' His brother laughed at his characteristic bluntness, but Thomas ploughed on. 'I think I want to continue in the church and be a deacon, or even a bishop.'

'Well, if that's what you want, I'm sure you'll get there. I don't think you've ever failed at anything you've set your mind to, Tom. And it's a well paid and comfortable job too. I'll definitely have to come and stay in your stately house during my shore leave!'

'I'm not doing it for the money,' Thomas protested, although he couldn't help but think that it did sound like a nice future.

'Well, I am!' John joked, 'so the pirates I catch better have chests filled with gold doubloons!'

'I'll send them a letter to make sure.' While Thomas' sense of humour wasn't as boisterous as his brother's, it was certainly still a healthy one!

***

St Paul's School in London turned out to be very different from Wisbech Grammar School. At 7 a.m. every morning, Thomas Clarkson filed into the three-tiered room, clutching a candle to light his way and shivering in the cool air. No fires were allowed at any time, even on the coldest winter day.

Thomas held his lesson book open with numb fingers, and began to re-read the pages the schoolboys had been told to memorise. At 7.30 a.m. the headmaster entered, dressed in black and rubbing his eyes.

'Right!' he called, his voice echoing in the huge chamber. 'Dickson, you're first!' As the boy stood up to recite, the headmaster tapped his cane on the stone floor. Everyone knew what the punishment was if they could not repeat the lesson.

The boy reciting at the front stuttered. The shadowy room, lit only by the huge wax taper in front of the headmaster, was silent. Every boy was watching, although Thomas knew very well what was going to happen next. It had been planned early that morning!

The headmaster lifted his cane as the unprepared boy ran out of words. At that exact moment a teenager at the front darted forward and blew out the headmaster's candle. The front of the room was plunged in darkness, and although the headmaster hit out with his cane, he was unable to see and kept missing as the boy dodged. Thomas smiled, but as the blowing-out-the-candle trick was a common solution when someone forgot their lesson, he was beginning to find the routine a bit frustrating!

While Thomas was not the most patient teenager in the school, he was certainly persistent. When the time came for him to enter Cambridge like his father, he had won several monetary prizes for academic achievement, and even had enough to keep a horse for hunting while at university.

Thomas didn't know it when he arrived at St. John's College, Cambridge, but if he had entered the year before, he would have met William Wilberforce, a man who would later become his close friend and fellow soldier in the fight against slavery. Thomas worked hard at university, and earned an honours degree with a first in mathematics. He was ordained as a deacon in Winchester and the year after won Cambridge's Latin essay prize.

'Look, Tom!' called a young man. 'Have you heard the announcement?'

Thomas looked up from his books. 'No?' Although already wearing the black robes which marked him out as a deacon, he was busy preparing for his Master's degree, the qualification necessary to become a vicar.

'Dr. Peckhard has released the Latin essay question. After winning last year, you must be going to try your hand at this one!'

'This one will be much harder, because it's for seniors,' interrupted another student. 'No one's ever won both Latin prizes.'

'I will.' Thomas stood up. He had not lost his habit of saying exactly what was on his mind. 'What is the question?'

'Anne liceat invitos in servitutem dare?' said the first student.

'Is it right to make slaves of others against their will?' translated the second.

Thomas remembered a sermon which Dr. Peckhard had given at the university. The vice-chancellor had criticised the African slave trade, on the basis that God had created all men free. He smiled, guessing that this was what Dr. Peckhard wanted the students to discuss. Confidence bubbled in Thomas' chest. He was good at Latin and gifted at research. He knew that if he worked hard he had a decent chance of winning this second competition, something which would ensure fine job prospects in the future.

There was only one problem. Thomas knew nothing about the African slave trade, and the essay was due in two months. Good thing he liked a challenge!

First Thomas wrote to his brother John, who, having been in the navy since turning thirteen, would be bound to know something about the trade. Surely he would have seen firsthand the slaving ships which brought men, women and children from the coasts of Africa to work in plantations in Jamaica and the West Indies.

Next Thomas visited several officers who had travelled to the West Indies and questioned them about what they had seen. It wasn't much – certainly not enough to write an essay on! Then John sent him a couple of pages of writing from a friend who had been to the West Indies – but it still wasn't sufficient.

'How's the essay going, Tom?'

'Not well.' Thomas replied, pacing restlessly in his friend's parlour. 'I've only been able to get a few tales from sailors – but I need numbers and statistics. How else am I to understand the slave trade enough to argue whether it's right or wrong?'

'That's true,' his friend said. 'We don't see slaves in England, not really. The ships go straight from Africa to the West Indies and exchange the slaves for the sugar, gin and cotton we need here. It's hard to believe it's as bad as Dr. Peckhard says. I'm sure the Africans are quite happy to travel outside of their country!'

Thomas wasn't listening. He had stopped in front of a table where that day's newspaper was spread open. An advertisement for a book caught his eye. 'Anthony Benezet's *Historical Account of Guinea*,' he read aloud. '*An Inquiry into the Rise and Progress of the Slave Trade, Its Nature and Lamentable Effects*. This is exactly what I need!'

'What? Tom? Where are you going?'

'London!' Thomas shouted, throwing the newspaper at his friend. He left Cambridge immediately, and soon succeeded in hunting down a copy of the book. Within its covers he found not only a lot of details about the slave trade, but also references to other books and articles on the same topic. These were very valuable to him because they were written by people who had not just witnessed but been personally involved in the slave trade.

Returning to the university, Thomas began to read all he had collected.

The more he read, the more his excitement faded. Could the terrible things written inside these books really be true?

A Life-changing Essay

'Tom?' A university friend poked him. 'Did you want to come out for a ride this weekend?'

'No, I'm working on my essay.'

'You need a break. You look exhausted.' It was true. Twenty-four years old and six feet tall with an athletic build, Thomas Clarkson did not often look so pale.

'I can't stop thinking about the slave trade,' Thomas admitted, rubbing his eyes on his black deacon's gown. 'I can't sleep. Even during the day I see the images described in Benezet's book. Children torn from their parents. Men and women tortured with whips and irons, forced to toil for long hours in the sun, and barely fed enough to survive. And the journey over in slave ships – it's unthinkable! Children as young as ten months old are beaten and chained for up to eighteen hours at a time. And all for what? So we can eat sugar and weave clothes from cotton? It makes me feel sick.'

Thomas' friend frowned. 'But surely slavery is biblical?'

'It is not!' Thomas thundered, rising to his feet. 'How can you say that? The Bible explains that on Judgement Day every person is to stand up and be accountable to God. Yet slavery means that one man can force another to do wrong, and sin against his Maker. Slavery cannot be right if it interferes in a man's relationship with God.'

'Alright!' Thomas' friend raised his hands. 'You're a fiery redhead Tom, that's for sure. But does it really matter if slavery is right or wrong? It's been around for ages. It's legal.'

'That doesn't make it right,' Thomas argued. 'As Christians we are called to treat other people as we would want to be treated! Do you want to be kidnapped from England and forced to work as a slave? Do you want to be starved and beaten and ...'

Thomas' friend left. He knew that once Tom Clarkson got started on a topic he was passionate about, there was no stopping him!

As the weeks passed and the essay deadline loomed, Thomas began to get more and more upset. The horrors of the slave trade were all he could think about. Each evening he left a candle burning so that if he had an idea in the middle of the night he could get up and write it down without wasting any time. Some nights he didn't sleep at all, tossing and turning, weeping over the awful things that were happening to his fellow humans across the seas.

'You really want to win this prize,' a friend commented one day.

'No,' Thomas said. 'All the joy I thought I'd have in writing this essay has gone. Now I just want to write a good argument which might in some way help poor Africa.'

At last the essay was finished. Thomas sent the paper to Dr. Peckhard and breathed a sigh of relief. Perhaps now he could forget all the horrors he had discovered and get some rest. But this was not to be.

Thomas won.

As was custom, he was called to publicly accept his award and read his essay in the Senate House at Cambridge University. On his way back to London, however, it was not the imposing, white building Thomas remembered, or the crowds and professors who had congratulated him, but the words he had read.

Hundreds of thousands of Africans were being horribly mistreated and not a single person he knew was doing anything about it.

As Thomas urged his horse along, his stomach began to shift uncomfortably. Surely it couldn't be true. Maybe he had made a mistake in his research. Perhaps he didn't really understand what was happening.

Too troubled to ride, Thomas slipped off his horse and began to walk. As his long legs strode down the road, he remembered the meticulous research he had done and the eyewitness accounts he had collected. As much as he wanted to, he could not convince himself he had made it all up.

Agitated, he threw himself down beside the road near Wadesmill, and dug his fingers into his thick, red hair. As his horse began to crop at the grass, Thomas came to a realisation. If everything he had written about the slave trade was true, someone had to stand up against it.

As he worked through his Master's degree over the next few months, this thought continued to haunt him. Thomas walked often in the woods, turning the contents of his essay over and over in his mind, hoping that eventually he would feel at peace. But instead the same question kept popping up. Is this true? Yes. Then someone must stop it.

But who? Thomas knew of no one who was as sickened by the slave trade as he was. But what could he do? He had no ability to change the laws of the country; he had no great wealth or influence. He was so young – it would be crazy to believe he could destroy the horrific trade.

Yet, Thomas slowly realised, there was one thing he could do. He could translate his essay into English and publish it. He could make the truth known.

'I'm glad you're doing this, Tom,' his brother, John, said, sitting back in his chair in their family house at Wisbech that winter. The table in front of them was spread with papers scrawled over with Thomas' neat handwriting and John's rather less-practised hand. For once Thomas' brother found nothing to joke about in the sobering information he was helping to translate.

'This is awful. I still can't believe that the captain of the ship *Zhong* threw 130 living Africans overboard in order to claim insurance. It's even more disgusting that the court ruled he was innocent of murder because Africans have no more worth in the eyes of the law than horses!'

'How can people who call themselves Christians do such things?' asked Thomas, firing up immediately. None of his passion over the injustices of the slave trade had left him. 'It's not right …'

John waited until his brother was finished, and then bit the feathery end of his pen. 'We've finished half your essay, Tom, and it's already come to sixty pages. Do you think it might be time to find a publisher?'

In January 1786 Thomas travelled once more to London. Navigating down the cobbled streets of Westminster, around gentlemen and ladies out for a stroll and sellers hawking various products, he made his way to the Strand. The busy thoroughfare was lined with printers and bookshops, but Thomas soon located the door of a well known publisher.

'Of course we can publish it,' Mr. Cadell said. He beamed at Thomas. 'It won first prize and so I will be able to sell it to many respectable people.'

Respectable? 'No, thank you,' Thomas decided. 'I don't wish it to be read only by respectable people, but by useful people, people who will be moved by what I have written and want to do something about it.'

Disheartened but resolute, Thomas decided to visit an acquaintance while he was in town. On his way there, he bumped into a family friend.

'Thomas!' Mr. Hancock exclaimed. 'You are just the person I wanted to see!' He pulled Thomas aside, the Royal Exchange bustling around them. 'I heard about your essay, why haven't you published it?'

Thomas blinked. 'Why are you concerned about publishing it?'

'I am a Quaker, as you know, and we have long been interested in putting a halt to the slave trade. Several of the Quakers are very interested in your work.'

'Then I would very much like to talk to them!' Thomas followed his Quaker friend down the crowded street, dizzy at this sudden turn of events. He was not alone in his hatred of slavery! There were others who felt the same way.

Thomas grinned. *Thank you for setting up this meeting, God!*

It may seem strange that Thomas had never heard of these others who were against the slave trade. Yet Quakers at this time were called 'nonconformists', which meant they were not associated with the main churches of the day. They dressed in dark colours, refused to address people using titles, and sought to distance themselves from the secular world as much as possible, believing it would help them grow in holiness.

Quakers didn't attend university and their opinions were not given much weight by most people. This didn't matter to Thomas. He knew that in Christ they were his brothers, even if they practised their Christianity differently.

In fact, Thomas soon discovered that he had more in common with the Quakers than his friends in the Church of England! Like them he dressed in dark colours, thinking fashion a waste of time. Like them, he paid little attention to differences in class and rank, and, unlike many people who attended church only because it was expected of them, he believed that your faith should impact every area of your life.

That same afternoon Mr. Hancock introduced Thomas to James Phillips, a Quaker printer and publisher. After a short discussion, Thomas found that James was as enthusiastic as himself about making his essay available to as many people as possible.

'Will you publish my essay?' Thomas asked.

'Yes,' said James, 'and I can help you with your improvements and additions too, if you like.'

When Thomas next met with James, he was introduced to several other Quakers. 'Why did you first write your essay?' one man asked.

'I wanted to win the prize.' Thomas said, always honest. 'All I wanted was honour – but writing the essay has changed me. I believe that as a Christian, I have to do something about the slave trade. I have to tell people.'

As Thomas and the Quakers talked, he became increasingly aware that God had led him to James

Phillips and his friends. Was God pushing him to be involved somehow in the destruction of slavery? Was such a thing even possible?

In June 1786, Thomas' essay was published by James Phillips. It was called *An Essay on the Slavery and Commerce of the Human Species, particularly the African* – and it was a huge success.

Thomas made the decision to personally deliver his book to individuals he thought were in a position to stand against the slave trade. He felt that since God had put him in touch with the Quakers, God would bless his efforts in this area also. And God did! Soon men and women with connections in literary, religious and political circles began to admit to Thomas that not only did they believe his essay, but they were willing to stand against slavery, even if by doing so they were laughed at or rejected by their friends.

It was while staying at the house of some of his new friends, that Thomas made a decision which would change the course of his life. Sir Charles and Lady Middleton lived at Teston Hall near green, sloping parklands. When he wasn't talking with them about slavery, Thomas spent long hours walking alone, thinking over all that had happened and all that he felt still needed to happen.

'I really must thank you, Reverend Clarkson,' Sir Middleton said, raising his drink. 'You have brought to public knowledge a great injustice which has passed almost unnoticed up until now.'

'Truly, to oppose a trade of human flesh is a worthy task of any man, and certainly the duty of every follower of God,' agreed another dinner guest.

Thomas put down his own cup. How happy it made him to know he wasn't alone in this immense task! What a blessing these companions were. 'It is indeed a worthy cause,' he said to the other guests, 'and one I am ready to devote myself to.'

'Well said, well said!'

'I salute you!'

'I am chairman of the Navy Board,' added Sir Middleton, 'and can help you obtain any naval records or accounts you may need regarding the African slave trade.'

Touched by the generous offer, and elated by the praises of the others, Thomas went to bed that night with a full heart – only to wake the next morning feeling worried. What had he done?

To pledge his complete devotion to such a huge undertaking was surely an act of insanity. Thomas dressed in a hurry and fled to the woods where he had walked alone so often. His doubts were numerous.

Did he have enough information, friends and money to attempt such a thing?

He remembered all the people God had so recently brought across his path, and their promises of support. He remembered the Quakers, many of whom were very wealthy, and hated the slave trade with a passion. Surely through these means God would supply all he needed.

But there was something which troubled him even more. Thomas was aware that if he were to devote himself to the abolition of the slave trade, it would mean giving his entire life to the work. It was no use if he wrote a book here or gave a speech there. The slave trade was a huge operation, and it would be a full-time job to oppose it. It may very well consume his whole life.

But who else could do it? All of his new friends, passionate though they were, had other jobs or tasks which took up their time. He, on the other hand, was just finishing his study and had not yet embarked on his church career. He was healthy, young and unmarried.

Here another doubt assailed Thomas. Was it a waste of his education not to begin a career in the church? He was ambitious and enjoyed studying. He knew he could become a famous bishop, and live a safe, comfortable life. He had a brilliant academic career ahead of him. Surely his family would be very disappointed if he gave this up, and – Thomas admitted to himself – so would he!

For two hours Thomas struggled in the woods.

Please show me the way, O God. I know that slavery makes you weep, and that you created all men to be free. For these reasons I know that the task of bringing down slavery is an honourable one. But it will be terrifying and difficult, and who knows if it is your will that I succeed?

As he knelt among the tree trunks, Thomas knew he could hesitate no longer. God was calling him to this and so he must do it.

'I will devote myself to the abolition of slavery.' He repeated his words from the night before, and this time he was certain that he meant them with all his heart and mind and soul. He had counted the cost.

As soon as he made the decision, Thomas' doubts fled. In fact he felt happier in that hour and in the days that followed than he ever had in his life.

What a beginning!

William Wilberforce

Down at the London docks the Thames was crowded with ships of all types and sizes. Boat masts pierced the white sky and dirty river water lapped against wooden, water-stained hulls. It was a bewildering new world of stretched ropes, bucking sails, and sailors speaking different languages. If only his sailor brother John were here!

Thomas found the ship he was looking for at last. It was a delicate trading craft called *Lively*, and Thomas had heard it regularly made trips to Africa.

'This is all from the coast of Africa, Captain Williamson?'

'That's right, Reverend.' The captain pointed out his wares one by one. 'That's ivory, and that's beeswax, very good stuff. Then we have pepper, palm oil, and wood to make into different dyes.'

'And this? Surely this has been spun in Manchester.'

'Not at all!' Captain Williamson picked up the pieces of beautifully woven linen. 'Made by Africans, in Africa, with African cotton.'

'It's very fine.'

Thomas left the ship with his arms full of samples of everything he had seen. How could people think Africans were no better than animals? Surely these works of art were concrete examples that such a belief was wrong.

The next vessel Thomas boarded was the *Fly*. Standing on the deck as it rose and fell, Thomas was conscious that hundreds of Africans had stood exactly where he was now. Men, women and children, created by God, but while he stood free, they had been weighed down with chains.

This was a slave ship.

Unlike *Lively,* the *Fly* had gratings on every window and entrance, and barricades across the deck. It was designed to keep men prisoner and prevent escape. Captain Colley took Thomas through a dark hatch door.

'This is where the slaves are kept on the voyage.'

Thomas looked around the dank space below deck. The roof was low and he could barely stand upright. Criss-crossing the currently bare floor were masses of chains and sets of manacles soldered into the timber. Today they were empty. During voyages they were not. The air smelt bitter and dirty. Was that dried blood smeared on the wooden columns?

'How ... how many hours a day are they kept down here?'

'Eighteen in good weather.' Captain Colley said. 'If the weather's bad it's too risky to take them out at all.'

'What about ...' Thomas couldn't finish his sentence. He was overcome by the thought of all the Africans suffered during the long slaving voyages. He thought of the starvation, the beatings, the chains which were never undone unless someone died, and even then sometimes only a few days later. Many, many Africans never made it to the West Indies. Thomas had written all this in his essay, but now he was seeing it with his own eyes.

'Anything else you want to see, Rev –'

'No!' He hurried back to the fresh air, shaking with horror and anger. 'I ... I must go.' Stumbling back along the docks, Thomas wasn't sure if he wanted to shout, cry or throw up. Surely there was nothing more awful in the entire world than this slave trade. It had to be stopped.

***

Thomas rubbed his eyes. Beside him Richard Phillips, cousin of James Phillips the publisher, yawned.

'Perhaps we should take a break.'

Thomas pushed away the muster rolls they were examining. The papers were filled with lists of all the British sailors who had sailed on a slave trading voyage and, as they read them, Thomas and James were discovering something fascinating.

Not only were slave voyages often fatal to the slaves themselves, but it seemed that one-fifth of all sailors also died – a much higher percentage than any other trade! Thomas knew that this information would be sure to concern the government, but he too was very tired and his eyes stung from the candle smoke. Busy with their various occupations during the day, Richard and he met every evening at 9 p.m. to work through the evidence, and a distant church tower had just chimed 1 a.m.!

'Brr ... It's freezing out here.' Richard thrust his hands into the pockets of his drab Quaker coat as they stepped outside. Thomas pushed his own hands into his very similar coat! They continued their circuit around Lincoln's Inn, the streets deserted and the night peaceful.

'I left a copy of my essay at William Wilberforce's house in Old Palace Yard, and today I received a letter. He wishes to see me.'

Richard nodded. 'I've heard he's claiming to have had a religious awakening. He's begun associating with other Christians, particularly those calling themselves "Evangelicals".'

'Exactly,' said Thomas. 'He's also a Member of Parliament and a brilliant speaker.'

'He sounds like the man we need if we are ever going to change the slavery laws,' remarked Richard. 'But for now, we have work to do!'

The two friends, invigorated by their brief walk, returned to the long lists of names. It wasn't until the bell tower tolled 3 a.m. that they finally parted ways.

***

'Ah, Reverend Clarkson, I must congratulate you on your essay!' William Wilberforce was an enthusiastic, friendly man, and Thomas liked him immediately.

'I must admit,' Wilberforce continued, 'that I have been thinking about the subject of the slave trade recently, and your essay came at just the right time. I have many questions.'

What followed was a long and demanding interview. Wilberforce was clearly considering the matter seriously. He wanted to know in detail all the evidence Thomas had collected and the names of witnesses so he could interview them himself. He was meticulous and thorough – two qualities which appealed very much to Thomas. Most importantly, he was a sincere Christian, believing with Thomas that God longed for all people to be free.

'You must visit me often,' said Wilberforce as Thomas finally stood to leave. 'I want to learn all you are discovering.'

Thomas wrote regular reports, and the two men met weekly, becoming firm friends over their mutual interest in the slave trade. Some evenings Thomas brought along other abolitionists and together they mulled over the best way to go about ending the trade.

It was all very promising, but as Thomas' Quaker friends reminded him: 'Mr. Wilberforce has not yet committed to bring the matter before Parliament.'

'I'll ask him this week.' Thomas promised.

'Reverend!' As Wilberforce welcomed him into his house, Thomas was suddenly beset by worries. What if Wilberforce said 'No'? If Wilberforce didn't bring slavery before Parliament then who would? His hands were sweaty, but knowing that hundreds of thousands of lives depended on the outcome to his question, Thomas opened his mouth.

And closed it again.

'Yes?' Wilberforce, only just over five foot, looked up at his tall friend and waited.

'Er ...,' Thomas swallowed.

'Yes?'

'It's ... it's nothing,' Thomas managed, and talk turned to other matters. When the time came to leave, Thomas still had not asked his important question. He returned to his lodgings, heart heavy. He would have to try again. *Please give me courage, God. Be with me and don't let me be overcome by fear.*

'Look, Thomas,' said Mr. Langton, a writer and abolitionist. 'Why don't I invite Mr. Wilberforce and some other gentlemen over for a party at my house? We can introduce the topic of the slave trade, and you ask him then.'

Relieved, Thomas agreed.

On the night of the party Thomas answered many questions both about his essay and recent investigations. He showed the guests his samples of cloth, and told them what he and Richard Phillips had discovered about the high rate of death among the sailors.

'Many planters in the West Indies say that the Africans are happier there than in Africa,' Mr. Boswell, another writer, said, 'but surely we have no right to make men happy against their will!'

Around the table men and women nodded and added comments of their own. In the midst of all the discussion, Mr. Langton asked Mr. Wilberforce whether he would take the issue to Parliament.

'I have no objection to it,' Wilberforce replied, 'once I am more informed, and if no one better suited to the job can be found.'

After dinner, Thomas took his friend Wilberforce away from the main gathering. 'May I tell my other abolitionist friends that you have agreed to bring the problem of the slave trade before Parliament?'

'You may,' Wilberforce promised.

Thomas left the party, feeling that this was the happiest day of his life! His joy only increased when shortly after, on 22nd May, 1787, he and twelve others joined together around a table in the Quaker printing shop and pledged to abolish the slave trade.

The Society for Effecting the Abolition of the Slave Trade was made up of men from all walks of life, Quakers and non-Quakers, young and old. Thomas looked around at each face, and felt that God had called each of them with their own individual gifts and talents to work together as members of one body.

What a great task lay before them!

***

One of the first things the Society decided was that Thomas should visit the other major British ports to collect more evidence. He agreed, deciding to ride rather than take a coach because it gave him greater freedom and privacy.

At first the journey was enjoyable, and provided him with some much needed time to think and plan, but as Thomas neared Bristol his spirits began to sink. Reining in his horse, he studied the mist-wrapped city and heard the church bells ring out eight o'clock in the evening. It was a haunting, sad sound, and Thomas swallowed.

How would people respond when they heard he was speaking up against the slave trade? Slavery brought their town so much wealth, and many relied on it for their daily bread. Thomas' hands shook as he held the reins, and he let his horse walk on.

I am doing God's work, he reminded himself. God had given him compassion for the slaves, and God would give him the courage and persistence necessary. After a while his fear began to pass, and when he entered the port his fingers had stopped trembling.

'Slave ships always have trouble getting sailors – they don't treat them well.'

'Did you hear of the slave ship that's just docked? Thirty-two sailors perished on that voyage.'

'See that tiny ship? It is designed to carry six passengers, but they regularly fit more than thirty slaves on board. The Africans can't even lie flat.'

Staring at the small ship, Thomas could hardly believe his ears. The rumours he heard at Bristol Port were so terrible that at first he thought they were being made up so the slave captains could prosecute him for gathering false evidence!

By interviewing sailors and other witnesses and checking their accounts against official records, Thomas soon realised that all the awful stories were true.

'Just through there, Reverend.'

Thomas climbed the narrow stairs, unsure what he would find. He had heard a shocking tale of a sailor who had been continually mistreated by his captain, and chained day and night on the open deck. After many inquires he had managed to find the man, and was hoping to get him to testify against the slave trade.

Thomas entered the room. On a narrow bed, a man lay tossing and turning feverishly. He was wrapped almost entirely in bandages!

'Good evening,' Thomas said. 'Do you mind if I come in?'

The man was too ill to answer so Thomas sat down beside him. 'Who did this to you?'

'My captain,' the sailor croaked. 'And the first mate. Have you been sent to finish me off?'

'No,' Thomas said, a lump rising in his throat. He kept his voice gentle. 'I've come to help. Can you tell me what happened?'

But the man was too sick to speak much that day, and before Thomas could return he received a message informing him the man had died.

***

'I want to take his captain to court for murder.'

A friend of Thomas who understood the law well, shook his head. 'There's no point. It's not an uncommon occurrence, and you would not be able to find witnesses because sailors never stay on land for very long.'

It was wise advice, but Thomas struggled to accept it. He knew that what he had seen was wrong. Using his indignation as fuel for his labour, he once again began to work until the early hours of the morning. When he finally did go to bed he lay awake, seeing before him the faces of all those who were suffering because of the slave trade.

'They get sailors drunk and then force them to sign a paper saying they will work for very little money. Other times they encourage them to get into debt, and then explain that the only way they can pay it off is to pledge to work on the slave ships.'

Thomas listened to the innkeeper at the Seven Stars. It was a rumour he'd heard many times in Bristol. 'I need to see this with my own eyes,' he said. 'Will you take me? It would be a kindness I'd never forget.'

The innkeeper looked the tall redhead up and down. 'Aye,' he agreed. 'Meet me here at midnight.'

That night and for eighteen nights afterwards, Thomas joined the innkeeper at midnight and followed him into loud taverns filled with dancing, drunken men. Again and again he watched as sailors were tricked into joining the slave trade and forced to sign contracts without reading them. Many would wake the next morning aboard a strange ship bound for Africa with no hope of escape. The sights he saw made bile crawl up Thomas' throat, but they proved beyond doubt that the rumours were true.

While it was not difficult to find people willing to talk about the slave trade in Bristol, it was almost impossible to find anyone willing to testify before Parliament. Thomas left each interview frustrated.

'You need to rest, Thomas, even if it's only for a few days. Go to Monmouth.'

Thomas shivered. Spending so much time outside and on the docks meant that he frequently spent the entire day in wet clothes. He still slept very little and his joints had begun to ache. He realised his new friends in Bristol were right.

'Only a few days,' he said.

His brief rest was rewarded, however, because when he returned to Bristol, his friends had exciting news. 'We found someone who might be willing to testify!'

Danger at Liverpool!

Thomas sat opposite Dr. Falconbridge, feeling very nervous. The ship's surgeon had been on four voyages to Africa, and was so distressed by what he had seen that he refused to have any more to do with the slave trade. He had told Thomas all he had witnessed of the mistreatment of both Africans and sailors. His accounts were invaluable, but Thomas had not yet asked him the all-important question: would the doctor be willing to swear to them before Parliament?

Over the next few days the two men met frequently, until at last Thomas felt he could ask. 'Doctor, are you willing to testify against the slave trade?'

Dr. Falconbridge sat up straight in his chair. 'Absolutely! I have left the horrible business and I will tell everything I know, to anyone you want, at any time you want. It must be brought to an end.'

At last, a witness! Thomas was so overwhelmed by joy that he felt quite weak and flopped back in his chair. 'Thank you. Thank you. You are a good man,' he said, 'and what you are doing is right in the eyes of God.'

For the rest of the day, Thomas found himself unable to settle to any of his usual jobs. He had a witness! Praise God.

***

'Please, Reverend Clarkson, you must help me,' the old woman said. 'My son William Lines, a sailor, was killed by the chief mate aboard his ship, but nothing has been done about it!'

Thomas was beginning to be well known in Bristol through his investigations. Mistreated sailors and their families often came knocking at his door, wanting a listening ear and justice.

'I've heard about your son,' Thomas said with a kind smile, 'but there were no witnesses.'

'I know of four,' William's mother said. 'Together we may be able to convince them to speak out. Will you take up the case?'

Thomas remembered the friend who had advised him against meddling in legal cases for individual sailors. Yet he had seen so much evil, surely he ought to be allowed to get justice for just one woman. Perhaps if he was successful, others would see and join him in the battle against slavery. 'We will go to court,' he told her. 'I'll do my best to get justice for your son.'

The courtroom was full of angry men who glared at Thomas as he entered. Some of the slave trade captains stood up to whisper to the mayor before the session began, probably hoping he would speak to the magistrate on their behalf. 'He's spreading false reports,' they said. 'Throw him out!'

Thomas took his seat and tried to remain calm.

'He wants to destroy our trade,' the men continued. They brought many other made-up accusations against Thomas. At last he could bear it no longer. Thomas stood up and looked his accusers in the eye. 'You sirs,' he said, 'may know many things that I do not. But I know this: if you do not do right in this earthly court, there is a Higher Court, and one day you will stand before it. What excuse will you give the Great Judge for what you do now?'

There was silence in the court. Thomas' accusers returned to their seats, and the session continued. Eventually it was determined that the case should be held in London before the Lords of the Admiralty.

'This trial will be continued at a later date,' said the magistrate, and closed the court.

***

'Thomas! I've been looking for you.'

'Can you believe that these things are sold in shops in your city?' Thomas waited for his friend to catch up, and then showed him the handcuffs, thumb screws and other instruments of torture he had just bought. 'I can use these as proof to those who think that Africans choose to be slaves. Why would they need handcuffs if that were the case?'

'That's good, but Thomas, we've just received letters from your Society in London.' His friend showed him the papers. 'You've been so focussed on your work here that you haven't written to them. They want to know if you're still alive!'

After writing to the Society of his progress, and reassuring them that he was, indeed, still alive, Thomas continued his travels. He passed through the towns of Gloucester, Worcester and Chester, and in each of these he found individuals who were willing to stand up against the slave trade.

'After all you've told us,' the editor of the Gloucester paper observed, 'I'm sure we can get many signatures on a petition to Parliament from this town alone.'

'Just wait,' Thomas cautioned, although he wished he could ask the editor to start collecting signatures immediately! 'I don't believe it's right to organise petitions until people know exactly what they are signing.' He remembered the sailors in Bristol who were forced into blindly signing work agreements for slave ships. 'Give out this summary booklet of my research to everyone who's interested. Make sure they have enough knowledge to judge for themselves what they believe to be right.'

Arriving at Liverpool, Thomas soon bought further beautiful specimens of African produce and art, as well as more horrific pieces of slave torture equipment. Both of these he packed away into a large crate for future use. Next time someone told him that slavery didn't exist, or that Africans were little better than animals, he had visible evidence which would prove them wrong.

'That's 'im! That's Thomas Clarkson.'

'Did you hear that he accused Captain Lace of murdering 300 Africans in Calabar?'

'He's come here to cause trouble, no doubt. Making up lies.'

Chewing his dinner, Thomas tried to ignore the whispers. He was sitting alone in the public dining room of the King's Arms Inn. He would be in the area for several weeks, collecting evidence.

'They've come in the hope of seeing you,' Dale the innkeeper told Thomas later that night. 'You've brought me many new customers!'

Soon however, the dining room crowds were no longer content to whisper and point. They began to try and provoke Thomas into an argument.

'I've heard there's a madman in town, come to destroy our glorious town of Liverpool.'

'It would be much better for that madman if he'd stayed safe at home.'

'Let's drink to the success of the slave trade!' All the patrons laughed and cheered. Thomas was the only one who didn't raise his glass. He was thinking furiously – what was the best way to deal with this situation? If he moved out and found lodgings at another inn it would look as if he were running away. If he stayed and discoursed with the men who came to argue with him, he might be able to better understand their arguments for slavery, and thus speak against them – yet there was always the danger he would lose his temper and bring shame to Christ and the Abolition Society.

Thomas chose to stay, but gave himself some guidelines: he would never personally start a discussion on slavery in the dining room, but he would never leave if the conversation started naturally. He would defend abolition seriously but without getting angry or irritated by his opponents, even when they insulted him.

These proved difficult rules to keep, and Thomas was soon very glad that Dr. Falconbridge had agreed to come with him.

'Ha! You're just making this up, Clarkson. You've never been to Africa!'

'But I have,' Dr. Falconbridge said, raising his head from his dinner. 'And I know that all he says is true.'

'Er, right then.' Thomas' opponent looked at the broad-shouldered doctor and took a step back.

Night after night, the redhead and the doctor defended their cause, speaking honestly and without ridiculing their opponents. As a result, many people began to understand the truth about slavery for the first time. Yet once again it proved difficult to find anyone willing to testify in Parliament.

'If I do, my house will get pulled down,' one man admitted.

'There are some men who have promised to hurt me and my family because I subscribed to your Society,' another said.

'You need to be careful, Reverend,' Dale the innkeeper said one evening. 'I want you to continue to stay here, but there are some men who are pressuring me to turn you out.'

'You've been kind to me, and I don't want to hurt your business.' Thomas said. 'I will rent a room in Williamson Square and see all my visitors there instead of in your dining room.'

Often, however, Thomas found that his witnesses were too afraid to visit, and more creative actions were required.

'I've found the perfect place,' Dr. Falconbridge told Thomas. 'There are two rooms in this tavern, separated by a wall with a small window. If you stand on a chair you will be able to see and hear the witness, but he won't know you're there.'

Thomas was trying to discover whether the rumours he had heard of a ship-board crime were true. If they were, they needed to be investigated, but the witness which was found refused to speak in front of Thomas, afraid his slave ship captain would punish him for doing so.

It turned out the room in which Thomas was to hide was one where bodies were stored before burial! Wobbling on top of a stool, ears straining to hear the conversation next door, Thomas tried to ignore the awful smell.

'Yes,' came the voice of the witness. 'That is all true. I saw it.'

As soon as he heard those words, Thomas leapt from his chair and rushed out of the room. Now he knew for certain the crime was true, he could investigate properly. Taking great gulps of fresh air, he was thankful that the witness' statement had come when it did. He wasn't sure how much longer he could have stayed in that stuffy, smelly room!

***

LEAVE LIVERPOOL OR WE'LL MAKE SURE YOU NEVER LEAVE.

Thomas showed the anonymous letter to Dr. Falconbridge, who frowned. 'You shouldn't walk out alone anymore, Clarkson. I will come with you everywhere.' And without telling Thomas, the doctor slipped a revolver in his pocket next time they left the inn. Liverpool was proving to be a dangerous place to be an abolitionist, as Thomas was about to find out.

***

The wind raced across the sails of the ships and the grey clouds rolled over Thomas' head. He and several others stood on the edge of the pier watching a group of small boats bobbing on the dark ocean. Out of curiosity Thomas had wanted to see the effect of the gale on the boats moored at the docks. Now, however, it was getting cold, and he turned to leave.

Eight men were coming down the pier towards him. Thomas kept walking, expecting them to break apart and let him pass. But they didn't. Instead they formed a line and marched onward, pushing him back towards the edge of the pier and the freezing, churning water.

Thomas stumbled, feet skidding on the rough wood. The end of the pier was very close now, two more steps and he would end up in the ocean. The wind tore at his coat, making it difficult to keep his balance. What were these men trying to do? He squinted at them through the gloom of the approaching storm, and recognised their faces straightaway. One, he knew, had murdered a fellow sailor, and two of the others had insulted him and Falconbridge at the King's Arms. At once Thomas understood their plan. If they threw him off the pier they could claim he had fallen accidentally during the storm, and get away with his murder!

'Let me go!' Thomas surged forward and tried to push the men out of his way. One fell down, and Thomas leaped over him towards safety. Hands grabbed at his clothes, and several fists connected with his body. Thomas pushed on.

'Leave Liverpool!' they shouted, calling him awful names as he sprinted towards mainland.

'That was a very close call,' Dr. Falconbridge said that evening as he dabbed at Thomas' battered head with a wet cloth. 'You could have lost your life.'

'After Lancaster, my next stop is Manchester. The mills there weave the cotton picked by slaves. I wonder how they'll receive me.' Thomas mused aloud. He would certainly need God's protection more than ever before.

***

'Reverend Clarkson! Welcome! We can't wait to hear what you have to tell us about the slave trade. We've been learning so much recently, and we're sure Manchester will be proud to present a petition to Parliament very soon.'

Thomas stared at the gentlemen who'd come to meet him on his arrival at the city. This was certainly very different to Bristol or Liverpool! 'But who has told you about the horrors of the slave trade?'

It turned out that while he'd been visiting Liverpool and the other ports, the Society back in London had been very busy spreading information throughout England, using pamphlets and articles. Thomas, with his usual single-mindedness, had been too busy to even pick up a newspaper since he had left London, and so had not known!

Once again grateful that God had not called him to fight slavery alone, Thomas swung himself down from his horse.

'Oh, we see you're a clergyman,' one gentleman said, as his black robes fluttered. 'You must preach on Sunday in our church. Speak to us about the slave trade.'

'But ... but Sunday's tomorrow!'

'Please, you must,' said another man. 'Nothing would please us more. Besides, we've already put posters up!'

As they continued to beg him, Thomas's face began to turn the colour of his hair. 'I'll ... I'll think about it,' he said finally. What should he do? It was Saturday afternoon, and it had been a very long time since he had preached a sermon. After all, he had given up his profession to pursue abolition. Writing a sermon was a serious, holy task and he didn't want to step into it lightly. He also wasn't sure if it was right to speak about political matters from a church pulpit.

He shared his doubts with his new friends, but they were not concerned. 'As Christians we have been called to love all men, so slavery is something we must talk about.'

The next day Thomas walked up to the pulpit, feeling hot in his robes, his neck sweaty. The church was completely full, each pew crammed with people who had come to hear him speak. Forty or fifty of the congregation were free black women and men who wanted to hear what the now-famous Thomas Clarkson would say about Africa.

Swallowing, Thomas opened his Bible.

'... God told the Israelites not to oppress the strangers among them. Jesus told us to show mercy to others as we have received mercy. We must apply these teachings to ourselves. The slave trade is a fact and can be proved. How can we come to church and pray to God and still oppress his children in Africa? How can we ask God to deliver us from evil, when we heap evil against our brothers and sisters?

'Instead, as servants of God, we must stand against this evil. With right motives, we must do all in our power to fight against the slave trade, even when people tell us slavery is good or right. If we do this, on the day the world comes to an end, we will be able to say that we have done our duty as Christians. We will be able to stand up without the stain of the African slave trade on our consciences.'

The packed church was completely silent as Thomas finished his sermon. His words had touched the congregation deeply. Like the Africans in North America and the West Indies, most of the inhabitants of Manchester also felt like strangers in a strange land. They had migrated from all over England to work in the new mills, and they knew what it was like to be uprooted from their homes and toil long hours in dangerous conditions. How much worse it was for the Africans who had no choice and were not paid for their labour!

Let the People be Heard

'Thomas! There you are!'

Thomas pulled his horse to a stop, surprised. He was passing through Bristol on his return journey to London, and had not expected anyone to be waiting for him.

His Bristol friend waved a letter. 'Haven't you seen the papers? The Lords of Admiralty sent you a letter, but you must have missed it. The case of William Lines, whose mother you promised to help, has gone to court in London – but none of your witnesses have turned up!'

The news landed like a punch in Thomas' stomach. His other friend in Bristol had warned him not to bring the case to court, because sailors never stay in one place – and he had been right. But Thomas couldn't give up now. What had happened to William Lines was wrong, and he had pledged to see justice served. Besides, if word got out that Thomas was unable to produce witnesses for this case and it was dismissed, his opponents might claim that what he had said about the slave trade was also a lie.

'Do you know why the witnesses haven't gone to London?' Thomas had hurried to the house of William's mother, heart racing with the unexpected news.

'Two of them were bribed by slave captains and have gone to sea,' the woman replied, untying her apron. 'The other two were good sorts, and decided they would go where they could not be tempted … so they've gone to work in a Welsh coal mine! I wrote to them, but I haven't received an answer. I don't even know if they got my letter.'

'We'll send someone to fetch them,' Thomas' Quaker friend reassured the redhead. 'If he rides all night, he might get there in time.'

Thomas spent the afternoon trying to find new witnesses, but it was useless. The two sailors in Wales were their only chance. He sat down to dinner, but found he could not eat. What if the messenger had run into trouble? It would have been better to send two young men. Finally he could stand it no longer, and got up from the dinner table.

'I'm going to follow the messenger,' Thomas said, once he found his Quaker friend. In the distance the clock tower chimed six in the evening. 'Perhaps I can help him. Or if he's gotten lost, I can fetch the witnesses myself.'

'But it's storming!' his friend protested. Thomas ignored him.

***

Thomas strode down to the River Severn, rain battering across his shoulders. It was almost dark.

'Who will take me across?' he called. 'I will pay well.'

The men at the boathouse shook their heads. 'We're not going out in that tempest,' they protested. 'We're not that mad.'

'I'll go if you give me three guineas,' laughed one, thinking Thomas would never pay such a large amount.

'I will,' promised Thomas, holding out a hand, 'but we have to leave now.'

Caught by his own words, the sailor had little choice but to get his boat. Once out on the river, the waves pushed and pulled against the small craft, tearing it in first one direction, and then another. Thomas held onto the shuddering wood with both hands, but even then he had difficulty keeping his seat. White foam splattered across the vessel, and the rain poured down from above. Soon they were all soaking wet.

'This is hopeless.'

'It's freezing out here.'

'We're almost there,' Thomas encouraged. In his heart he wasn't so sure. Would they really make it? *Please God, keep us safe*, he prayed. What little food he had eaten began to roll over in his stomach.

'We're lost! This is all your fault,' hissed the sailor.

'I didn't force you,' protested Thomas. 'Look! Is that a light?'

It was. They steered towards it and ten minutes later they landed on Welsh soil, very grateful to be alive. Then Thomas made a discovery. The light had not been lit to guide ships at all. Rather, God had planned for a maid servant to stop for a conversation on the staircase near a window, and the light had been the candle in her hand! At the very moment when they needed direction, light had shone out of the darkness.

'Go to bed for now, and we'll dry your clothes,' said the people at the boathouse.

Thomas had little choice but to agree. It was near midnight, and he was shaking all over, and not just with cold. His cheeks were hot and flushed. 'Wake me up as soon as they're dry,' he made them promise.

They woke him at two in the morning, and Thomas ate a meal by the fire, trying to get as warm as possible before he had to venture out into the storm. The next part of his journey was long and lonely, but when Thomas finally caught up with the messenger, he was overjoyed – the young man had found both sailors!

They travelled back to the boathouse together, arriving exactly twenty-four hours later, at two in the morning.

'Absolutely no boat is going out on the river tonight. It's a miracle you were able to cross earlier. There are no horses either. You'll have to go to bed.'

The two witnesses, the young messenger, and Thomas were able to cross to Bristol the next morning. By now Thomas was very ill. His throat was scratchy, his head pounded, and his fever had returned. Unable to travel any further, he handed the witnesses letters of introduction, and gave them over to the care of William Lines' mother, who accompanied them to London.

After such dramatic events, the next letter Thomas received about the trial was very disappointing. Lying in bed, aching all over, Thomas read that the witnesses had been too late by only a few hours, and the case had been dismissed. The murderous chief mate had been set free.

Oh God, prayed Thomas, collapsing against his pillow. *Please let the chief mate be aware of his narrow escape, and let him turn to you in sorrow for what he has done. Use this situation to save him.*

After this Thomas resolutely turned his attention to getting well and the next steps in his campaign to end slavery.

***

'Welcome back, Clarkson!'

Thomas grinned. After five months it was good to see his abolitionist friends again, but as always, there was work to do.

'The Society was wondering whether you could prepare a second edition of your essay, and add to it the facts you've uncovered during your travels.'

Tired, but having recovered from his illness, Thomas agreed. 'I'll go back to Wisbech and write it there. I've had enough of large cities for a while.'

'You did some marvellous work on your travels, Thomas. I heard one man say that hearing you talk about the evils of the slave trade was like hearing the apostle Paul speak to the crowds in Ephesus!'

Thomas shrugged the praise away. 'The Society has been very busy while I've been gone,' he said. 'I saw evidence of your work in the willing reception I received in Manchester.'

'We've sent out five hundred circular letters to inform people about the slave trade and the Society's goal to end it. We've got another one thousand letters at the printers, and we hope to soon have allies in over thirty-nine countries. The abolitionist societies in North America and France have already contacted us. In England, not only the Quakers, but the General Baptists have joined the cause, and several Church of England clergymen have sent letters promising their support as well.'

Thomas couldn't help but smile when he remembered how alone he had felt that day in the woods, and how impossible the task had seemed. Now God was raising up help from all directions, almost faster than anyone could count!

'... and here's a letter from the Methodist John Wesley,' the Society member went on, handing Thomas a piece of paper. 'It's just one of the many encouragements that are being sent to us daily.'

'I commend you to Him, who is able to carry you through all opposition,' Thomas read, 'and support you under all discouragements.'

How true Wesley's words were, and how true they would prove to be.

***

'So you're wearing jewellery now, Tom,' John laughed. 'That's a change! I'm not sure the colour matches your dark clergy robes though.'

Thomas was too excited about this latest invention from the Abolition Society to respond to his brother's teasing. 'It was a gift from the potter, Josiah Wedgwood. He offered to commission an engraver to create a seal to represent the Society. Like my box of chains and samples, it's a visual reminder to everyone that slavery is not right.'

John, serious now, picked up Thomas' personal medallion, engraved on a large orange carnelian crystal. A kneeling African in chains was etched in black on a white background. He had his hands raised, begging, and around him were the words, 'Am I not a man, and a brother?'

'It's very striking,' John agreed. 'And I recognise that phrase! It's from the title of the anti-slavery sermon preached by the university doctor who set the question for your essay.'

Thomas, refilling his pen, nodded. His fingers were sticky with ink from working on the edits for the second edition of his essay.

'But are many people buying them?' John returned the medallion. 'Are they popular?'

'Oh yes!' Thomas paused with his pen above the page. 'We've had thousands made. Men are having the seal inlaid with gold to put on their snuffboxes. Women are wearing it on bracelets and hairpins. For once,' he said, 'fashion is actually serving some useful purpose – the promotion of justice.'

'I'll have to get one for myself,' John said, grinning at his brother's dismissal of popular fashion. 'And for Mother.'

'That won't be difficult,' Thomas replied, adding a line of writing to his already full page, and nodding towards his bags. 'I brought five hundred with me.'

***

After finishing the additions to his essay, Thomas began to write a new book, calling it *An Essay on the Impolicy of the African Slave Trade*. He wanted to show that not only was the slave trade morally wrong, but it also did not benefit those who practised it, because one in five sailors died during slaving voyages. That meant there were more deaths in a single year from a slave ship, than in two full years from any other trade. In fact, more sailors died during the voyage than slaves because their captains knew they could not be exchanged for money at the end.

Thomas dedicated the book to his new friend William Wilberforce, but before he could finish it, he received a letter from Wilberforce himself.

'John! I have to leave for London immediately.' Thomas strode through the house, gathering up handfuls of letters and loose pages. As he wrote regularly to over four hundred correspondents, mountains of paper seemed to grow around him wherever he was.

'Why? What is it?' John stood up and began to help him pack.

'The King has heard that people are interested in the question of slavery. Parliament has informed him of the letters and petitions which are being sent in. As a result he has created a special council to examine the evidence for and against the slave trade.' Thomas swept the contents of his desk into a bag which already held far more books than clothes. 'This is the first step towards Parliamentary abolition, John!'

'Isn't Wilberforce already in London?' John saved the ink pot from falling over. 'Can't he provide the council with the evidence?'

'Wilberforce is very ill.' Thomas ran a hand through his hair. 'He's had to retire to Bath to rest, and he's written to ask if I can get the evidence ready and present it to the council.'

Three days after the beginning of the King's inquiry Thomas arrived in London.

'Prime Minister.'

'Ah, Reverend Clarkson. Wilberforce wishes me to speak to you. He says you have collected a lot of information about the slave trade.'

William Pitt was a friend of William Wilberforce, and being only a year older than Clarkson, he was the youngest Prime Minister England had ever had.

Thomas Clarkson shook the twenty-nine-year-old's hand and launched into a description of his recent journey and discoveries. The two men spoke for a long time. Like many people, Pitt had trouble believing the slave trade was that bad.

'If slaves are valuable, why would their masters mistreat them?'

'How can it be possible that so many sailors die?'

'If Africa truly does have great natural wealth, and a means of trade besides slavery, why haven't we all heard about it before?'

'Tomorrow,' Thomas promised, 'I will bring you all my samples, my notes and my books.'

William Pitt was very thorough. He looked through all the notes, and read Thomas' lists of the 20,000 seamen who had suffered greatly from being involved in the trade. Each name had been meticulously researched and verified, so as to prove the statistics were correct. Pitt examined the African wares, picking them up and turning them over in his hands.

'Thank you, Reverend, thank you,' he said to Thomas at last. 'You have shone a light in the darkness of this trade, and I understand now what I did not before.'

After this meeting, Pitt promised Thomas that he would make sure the evidence against the slave trade received a fair hearing at the council inquiry. Together with the rest of the Society, Thomas continued to visit MPs and encourage and equip them to speak out against slavery. He also began to gather together the witnesses willing to speak up against the slave trade, so they would be ready when called upon. Unfortunately, there weren't many.

'John Newton will speak before the council,' a member of the society confirmed. 'And his book, *Thoughts Upon the African Slave Trade*, is sure to move the hearts of many people.' This book was a detailed eyewitness account. John Newton, before he became both a Christian and a preacher, had spent many years as the captain of a slave ship. His story, like his hymn, *Amazing Grace*, is a testimony to the fact that God can change the hardest of hearts.

'One hundred and three petitions!' Thomas crowed, gazing at the paper covered table in the House of Commons. 'Nothing like this has ever been attempted before. All of England is rising up against the slave trade, and the people are clamouring to be heard! Petitions are the way of the future.'

The Society of Abolition agreed. They campaigned for a special petition just for the city of London, and sent a letter to the mayor of every English town which had not sent its own petition into Parliament.

***

'Thomas! Have you seen this?'

Thomas took the newspaper from his friend, and read aloud. '... after due examination it appears that the major part of the complaints against the Trade are ill-founded.' He stared, unable to believe his eyes.

'But the King's Council has only been looking at the evidence for a month! How can they make such a claim?'

'We need more eye-witnesses,' his friend replied. 'Particularly after that sailor who promised to tell the truth betrayed us at the inquiry and told lies about the slave trade and how 'happy' the slaves were.'

William Pitt, now passionate about abolition; his fellow MP Grenville; and the Bishop of London sent a letter to the Society. 'Quick! Get four witnesses ready to speak before the Council.'

Dr. Falconbridge honoured his promise to Thomas and spoke out bravely against the slave trade. Yet still the King's Council remained unconvinced. There were simply too many people willing to lie about the slave trade and too few people brave enough to tell the truth.

'It doesn't help,' observed one of the Quakers, 'that their witnesses are all men of high-standing, and most of ours are men in less respected professions. I've heard people say that only poor ruffians support abolition.'

'It's not right!' Thomas slammed a fist down on the table. 'Even men who claim to be Christians can't find the courage to testify. Does their faith mean so little to them?'

'It's a pity those two Swedish gentlemen can't help. They've come so recently from Africa that all they've seen would be fresh in their minds.'

'Swedish gentlemen?'

'Yes, I can introduce you, if you like.' Thomas' friend led the way through the crowd. 'Dr. Spaarman and Mr. Wadstrom are associated with the Royal Academy at Stockholm in the departments of medicine and precious metals.'

Thomas Clarkson shook their hands, almost trembling with excitement. Could these two men be God's answer to their lack of witnesses? 'I heard you've spent some time in Africa recently,' he said, getting straight to the point.

'Yes, our late king wished us to make discoveries in botany and mineralogy in Africa. The French government allowed us to visit the French colonies, including Senegal, and now we are on our way home to Sweden. We have seen many surprising things.'

They showed Thomas intricate specimens of African produce, and also their diaries where they had written detailed accounts of their journey, as well as all they had seen and heard about the slave trade.

'Will you share your testimony with the King's Council?' Thomas asked, praying they would say yes.

'Of course,' said Dr. Spaarman. A confident, well-educated man who had no personal interest in the slave trade to sway his judgement, the Swedish Professor was the perfect witness.

Surely this time the King's Council would have to change their mind about the slave trade.

Running out of Time

'Wilberforce is too ill to come to Parliament. His mother has just written from Bath; he's not even well enough to read our letters.'

'William Pitt says it's too late in the year to bring the matter of the slave trade before Parliament.'

'The King's Council are going through the evidence, but the slave traders are trying to delay the process so we won't get our turn this session.'

Thomas Clarkson watched in dismay as all their hard work began to crumble to the ground at the beginning of 1788.

'We must speak to individual Members of Parliament,' decided the Society, 'perhaps they can bring the matter straight before Parliament before it closes for the summer.'

'Mr. Fox,' Thomas said, 'will you speak up for abolition in Parliament during this session?'

For a long moment the Honourable Charles Fox was silent, and then he sat back and looked six-foot Thomas in the eye. 'Absolutely,' he said. 'The slave trade must be stopped!'

On 9th May, Mr. Fox introduced the matter of the slave trade to Parliament for the first time. The debate that followed was intense.

Fox's friend Edmund Burke stood up and agreed that it was important for every man in the House to understand the matter before them, because if they continued to rely on others to decide what was right, England would be plunged into moral darkness.

Sir William Dolben, MP for Oxford University, argued that something had to be done in this Parliamentary session, because he had calculated that otherwise ten thousand lives would be lost over the Summer vacation.

After much talk, Parliament decided that while there was not enough time to address the abolition of the slave trade, an act could be passed to try and lessen the horrors of slave voyages. It was called the Dolben Act, after the MP who fought for it, and was the first bill of law to ever be passed against the slave trade.

'It was the best we could hope for in such a short amount of time,' Thomas said, 'and even then, William Pitt had to threaten to resign in order to get it passed. But although slave ships are now limited in the number of Africans they can have on board, all those Africans are still destined for slavery.'

The Parliamentary battle for abolition had only just begun.

***

'I speak,' said Thomas, standing before the King's Council with his box of evidence, 'as a feeling witness to the sufferings of the African people. I have undertaken a difficult and unpleasant task, and I do not wish to deceive you.'

Shortly afterwards Parliament closed for the Summer. Thomas finished his book against the African slave trade, and the Society for Abolition met once again. Since their first gathering eighteen months before, the members had held fifty-one meetings, most of which were five hours long!

They had also published over 51,000 books and pamphlets, doing everything possible to bring the issue of slavery before the public eye. In doing so they had made formidable opponents, and knew that when Parliament opened once more, they would have to fight harder than ever to be heard.

'More witnesses, that's what we need. Will you ride again, Clarkson?'

'First,' Thomas replied, getting out a fresh piece of paper and beginning to draw up a neat table, 'I want to equip our supporters across the kingdom to find witnesses themselves. I cannot visit every town, but thanks to our publications we now have friends of abolition throughout the country.'

Thomas, thorough as always, ended up with 145 questions sorted neatly into six categories! The Society printed this list on a small slip of paper and sent it out to their correspondents. Now other abolitionists could interview potential witnesses, sending the answers via post back to the Society, who would determine whether the witness could be useful for the inquiry.

Once again, Thomas set off on his horse, this time to the south of England, from Kent to Cornwall. Surely after the petitions which had been sent in from all over the country he would be welcomed gladly by the people.

But this was not the case.

'You mad man! Leave us alone!'

'You're nothing but a ruffian and a meddler!'

In London talk of the slave trade was on everyone's lips. Gentlemen lost money at card games in clubs because they were so busy arguing about it that they forgot to play! Outside of the capital however, Thomas met the working men who could not afford to lose money on cards – and feared that the abolition of the slave trade would mean the loss of their incomes. In each town there were many who treated him coldly and insulted him. It seemed the abolitionists truly did have more opponents than before.

Yet there was something which Thomas found more frustrating than open hostility: questioning a reluctant witness. Men often agreed to be interviewed, and then as soon as Thomas dipped his pen into his ink pot and they realised their testimonies were about to become official evidence, they would change their minds and refuse.

Halfway through his journey, after the simple act of taking out his pen lost him many promising witnesses, Thomas discovered a solution. If he memorised his 145 questions, he wouldn't need to bring any papers with him, and if he wrote the answers down as soon as the interview was over he would not scare anyone else away with the presence of his ink pot!

'And how many voyages to Africa have you sailed on?' Thomas leaned back and took a drink from his cup. As someone who was used to speaking bluntly and often got quite passionate about the injustices he heard, he was having to learn to weave his questions into the conversation with tact and patience.

It was slow work, but Thomas was determined to do everything possible to put the person he was questioning at ease. Once he had questioned a witness in this casual manner, he would spend days tracking down the witness' family and friends.

'Will you convince your brother to testify to the slave trade?' he would ask. He had found that the witness was far more likely to agree to speak before Parliament if a family member asked.

After two months of travelling over 1,600 miles, questioning forty-seven potential witnesses, Thomas was rewarded with just nine who agreed to be examined by Parliament. While this was very disappointing, Thomas reflected that he had learnt a lot.

He had seen firsthand that it wasn't just the slave traders who were sinful. Ordinary men and women, even Christians, were able to convince themselves that money and comfort were more important than justice or kindness.

He had also seen that there were individuals who despite the pressure to ignore slavery, were willing to stand up and fight against it at great cost to themselves.

Thomas was also able to acknowledge that although it felt like his journey had been a failure, he could take comfort in the fact that he had done his duty under God. It was his Heavenly Father that he was working for, and he had given his best.

Lastly, even though he had found only nine witnesses, he had still collected much information on the slave trade and this might prove to be helpful in the future.

***

'While you've been gone we've also managed to find one or two men willing to testify,' a member of the Society reported when Thomas returned to London.

'My health has much improved,' said Wilberforce, 'and I have found a couple of witnesses too.'

Once again, Thomas was reminded of God's power. His own journey may have been largely unsuccessful, but God had provided the witnesses they needed from other places. However, this was not to mean the investigation would proceed smoothly! After only one of their witnesses had been sent to the King's Council, the King fell ill, and the hearing was suspended.

'Oi, Clarkson! There's a new ship at the docks, straight from Africa!'

Thomas immediately put down his papers and fetched his coat. He never missed an opportunity to gain fresh samples for his box of specimens. His large crate was now divided into four sections. One with various pieces of African wood; the second with other items such as ivory, musk, pepper, seeds and fruits; the third with an African loom, woven bags, gilded jewellery, glazed clay pots and other works of art; and the fourth with the shackles, thumb screws, neck collars and other instruments of torture used on slaves.

All of these Thomas was allowed to show to the King's Council when they began meeting once more. 'It is evident,' he said to the assembled men, 'that Africa has many other valuable items of trade besides men and women. If we abolished the slave trade we would not lose money, and we would save lives.'

'I can't believe it!' A member of the Society said to Thomas shortly afterwards. 'Our opponents have been able to interview every single one of their witnesses, and the King's Council has just written to say we are only allowed three!'

Thomas rested his head in his hands and let his shoulders slump. All the miles he had ridden and all the effort the abolitionists had put in to find as many witnesses as possible, and now they were only allowed three. It wasn't fair, but there was nothing he or the

Society could do. He raised his head. *Please, God, let three witnesses be enough.*

'I'll write to three immediately,' he told his friend, 'and tell them to come to London.'

***

'Tom! There you are, I just got back from Africa yesterday. I wrote down everything I saw, and I think I've got some good evidence here!'

'John!' Thomas beamed to see his brother again after his most recent voyage, but it was a smile tinged with regret. 'If only you had landed earlier! Our witnesses have just been examined, and we're not allowed anymore.'

John squinted against the candlelight. It was very disappointing to hear that his fresh eye-witness accounts would be useless, but he thought there was something else affecting his brother. 'Tom, have you been sleeping?'

'Not really.' Thomas slumped back in his chair and rubbed his short red hair. He'd taken off the grey wig, which, like many gentlemen at the time, he often wore when out.

'Is it all the work you're doing?'

Thomas considered the question. He was certainly very busy. He attended Society meetings weekly; looked after the witnesses who came to London to testify and made sure they were ready for the Council at the right times; travelled over 200 miles a week to corroborate evidence or hunt down new witnesses for future examinations; and wrote ten or twelve long letters a day in correspondence with yet more potential witnesses.

'No,' Thomas said eventually. 'I am busy, but it's not the work which is keeping me up at night. It's the eye-witness accounts I hear. I often have no time to read the written testimonies which are sent to me until almost midnight. Then I read of the awful sufferings of the African men, women and children, and I weep, John. After that I pace up and down my bedroom and swear that I will never stop fighting against this trade until it is utterly destroyed. So I sit back down and answer the letters until my eyes are too sore to see any longer, and then I go to bed.'

'To sleep?'

'No.' Thomas closed his eyes. 'To toss and turn and wake up because I see the slaves in their chains in front of me. I see their faces and their blood, and when I rise in the morning, they are still there in front of me.'

'Oh, Tom.' His brother, John knew, felt the sufferings of others very deeply. This was not wrong, after all, Jesus had wept over the city of Jerusalem, but it was painful.

'The happiness of millions depends on the work we do today, and tomorrow and the day after that,' Thomas said, as he farewelled his brother at the door. 'I really believe that this is the time for abolition. God has given me and others this passion, and he will use it.'

***

'Here's the final sketch, Clarkson.' James Phillips slid the large piece of paper over the table towards his friend. 'Do you think it's ready to print?'

Thomas picked up the sheet. On his latest journey to Plymouth, Thomas had managed to get his hands on the floor plan of a slave ship. This had given the Society accurate figures for the space given to each slave, and they had applied this ratio to the ship *Brookes* which docked at Liverpool.

'Four hundred and eighty-two,' murmured Thomas. That was how many tiny people were drawn in the diagram. The Dolben Act was supposed to reduce that figure to 454 – yet on its last voyage the *Brookes* had carried 609!

'Absolutely no room to move, let alone lie down flat,' agreed James.

'This picture will prove once and for all that our opponents are lying when they say the voyage from Africa to the West Indies is the happiest time of an African's life!' said Thomas.

The *Brookes* diagram was published in April 1789, and was an immense success. Like the Wedgwood carving of a kneeling slave, it was a visible reminder of the horrors of the slave trade. Many abolitionists bought a copy to hang in their drawing rooms, and African slavery quickly became a popular tea-time conversation topic throughout England. The issue could be ignored no longer, and instead the British population was forced to choose a side: Were they for, or against, abolition?

***

'Eight hundred and fifty pages long?'

At last the King's Council had finished hearing the evidence, and had announced that the subject of the slave trade was now ready to be brought to the House of Commons. There was only one problem – the Council's report was 850 pages long, and the Parliamentary debate was scheduled in three weeks' time!

'Right, gentlemen,' said William Wilberforce to Thomas Clarkson, James Ramsay and Dr. William Burgh of York. 'I have here four copies of the report. In order to represent our cause as thoroughly as possible, I need to understand and reference as much of this evidence as I can.'

The four men got to work. Each took a section of the report to read, and condensed it into notes Wilberforce could use during the debate. Every day for three weeks they met at dawn and toiled until late in the evening, reading, writing and reasoning. Beneath their pens, the immense collection of evidence slowly transformed into a tool Wilberforce could wield in Parliament.

Thomas' section was the treatment of sailors and the possibility of a produce-based trade with Africa. As well as this he managed to find the time to prepare and preach a sermon for Ramsay's church. James

Ramsay, was an ex-ship surgeon who, after witnessing the slave trade firsthand, had become a Church of England minister and abolitionist. Only fifty-five years old, he struggled with ill health, but refused to reduce the hours he was spending fighting for the freedom of Africa. A friend of the Middletons, at whose house Thomas had pledged his life to abolition, Ramsay had been part of the campaign from the beginning.

Meanwhile, the pro-slavery merchants from Liverpool and Manchester swarmed into London and held rallies on the streets. They did their best to convince the population that the abolitionists were lying, and their diagrams and facts were false.

On 12th May, William Wilberforce stood up in the House of Commons to deliver his first speech against slavery. While he had managed to read the notes his three friends had helped him make, there had been no time left to write a speech of his own!

'You cannot even imagine the amount of misery these little slave ships carry. So much suffering condensed into so little space,' he thundered. The Members were silent. 'Nothing short of absolute abolition is possible. We owe this to Africa, and we owe it to our own moral character!'

Wilberforce sat down, leaving many in the House impressed with his well-reasoned, well-spoken arguments. He had spoken for three-and-a-half hours. The Parliamentary debate against the slave trade had begun.

Adventures in France

'Never before,' said Thomas, 'has the House of Commons been so rowdy! The Speaker has to continually interrupt to keep order because both sides are so passionate.'

Despite this, the Parliamentary year concluded without any relief having been achieved for those in slavery. Instead, James Ramsay, whose health had grown worse, and who had been attacked by the newspapers for being a stout abolitionist, passed away. He sent his friend Thomas a letter just before he died.

'I am very unwell,' he wrote, 'but I take comfort in my faith, and the knowledge that I have not lived in vain, because abolition is worth fighting for.'

***

What should I do now, God? The death of his friend and the failure of Parliament to overturn the slave trade left Thomas very upset. After a time of mourning, he decided that the best thing he could do was make sure the abolitionists were as prepared as possible for the next Parliamentary session.

'We need fresh evidence, and more witnesses.' Thomas said. 'I'm going on another journey.'

The Society agreed, but Thomas had only just set out on his horse when he received a letter from Wilberforce calling him back to London.

'There has recently been much unrest in France: the population are campaigning for equal rights and freedom for all. Since they're currently so concerned about the poor, they ought also to be interested in the plight of Africa. I have spoken to the Society, and we agree that now might be a good time to encourage France to abolish the slave trade. If France passes a law about abolition, England might too!'

Thomas agreed instantly. He would do whatever it took to end the slave trade.

'But Clarkson,' a concerned friend protested. 'Paris is really quite dangerous right now. There have been riots. They've stormed the huge French prison, the Bastille.'

'I think it would be best if you went under a different name,' another friend agreed. 'You've become quite well known and your writings have been published in French. If it's too risky for Wilberforce to go, it would be safer if you pretended to be someone else.'

Thomas, always honest and straightforward, didn't like this idea. It seemed too deceptive, as if he had something to hide. The Society agreed with him, and so he boarded the boat to Calais under his own name.

'What precautions should I take against the robbers?' Thomas asked as soon as he landed on French soil. Ever since the fall of the Bastille, the English papers had been full of reports of robbery and murder.

The driver of the horse-drawn carriage lifted his eyebrows. 'There have been no such things around here, monsieur,' he said. 'It is safe, quite safe.'

And while Clarkson did arrive in Paris without being burgled, he still saw a lot of surprising things along the way! Everywhere he looked revolution flags hung, their red, white and blue pendants flickering in the breeze. Those he met wore colourful badges and talked excitedly about freedom, but there were less cheerful signs too.

'As soon as I get down from my carriage, whether I am in a village or a bigger town, I am instantly swamped by beggars. The poor are everywhere. They look miserable, and are in desperate need.' Thomas reflected. 'They also bow down at shrines to Mary on the side of the road, but they don't understand the gospel. I can't wait until the day when the French are able to look into their faith properly and receive answers to their questions.'

Thomas also enjoyed a tour of a prince's decadent mansion. The rich prince and many other aristocrats had fled the country, afraid of the people they had oppressed for so long. In Paris, Thomas found fire-eaters, dancing bears and troupes of actors! Following the celebrating crowd through the streets, he arrived at what was left of the Bastille. Workmen and tourists were tearing the old prison apart stone by stone, throwing the boulders into ditches with shouts and whistles. Thomas decided to take the opportunity to wander through the tiny cells which had held so many prisoners for so many years, often unjustly. In one cell he found a stone with an inscription in Latin and stopped to read what had been scratched there. The name of the prisoner was unreadable, but the next part was clear: '[name] wrote this line in the anguish of his heart.'

'Pardon,' Thomas said to two nearby workmen, 'Could you pull this stone out for me? I'd like to take it back to England.'

'Of course, monsieur. That is no problem at all.'

Not knowing that the French Revolution would result in the needless loss of many lives, Thomas was supportive of what he saw. The poor people in France, just like the Africans in the French colonies, were made in the image of God, and ought to be treated with justice and respect. By denying them freedom and education, the French rulers were limiting the spread of the gospel. Yet it was only the love of Jesus which could change their anguished hearts into joyful ones!

'Since the National Assembly is now ruling France, we will apply to the National Assembly for the abolition of the slave trade!' Monsieur Brissot de Warwille declared. A fervent abolitionist, he had become known as the 'Clarkson of France'! Like Thomas, he dressed simply in the manner of the Quakers; cared deeply about injustice; and believed every man in the world was his equal and his brother.

Thomas looked around the room. The number of abolitionists in France was few, but compared to England many of them were individuals of influence. Women also sometimes served alongside their husbands. Marquis de la Fayette, who had fought in the American Revolution, was keen to see the injustice of slavery removed and had begun to free the slaves on his own plantation. Surely the president of the National Assembly would listen to such distinguished men, and give Thomas the chance to speak and show his samples.

'Any news?'

'None.'

Day after day passed, and no message from the president came.

'Maybe the president does not wish to introduce the topic of slavery when there is already so much unrest.'

'Perhaps our letters have been intercepted and destroyed.'

'Have you seen the anonymous messages I have received?' A French abolitionist pulled out a handful of papers and spread them out on the table for the rest of the committee to see.

'Dissolve your committee or you and your friends will be stabbed. Signed: 300 enemies of abolition.'

Thomas glanced over at the letters and shrugged. 'Don't fear, I have received similar ones.' He pulled out the letters which had arrived at his residence over the last few days. 'Ah, there we go. The handwriting is the same! It seems we have made some wicked enemies.'

A few days later the newspapers were filled with lies about the Anti-Slavery Committee. One of them said that the abolitionists wished to send 12,000 guns to the Africans in St. Domingo so all the slave owners could be removed.

'As if we have 12,000 guns!' exclaimed a Committee member at their next meeting. 'How ridiculous.'

Knock. Knock.

The Committee members looked at each other. 'Everyone is here at the meeting. Who is that?'

Bang! The door to their meeting room swung open, and in crowded an entire guard of soldiers. 'We're here to seize all of your weapons!'

Thomas watched as the soldiers stamped up and down the room, looking into cupboards and chests. The search didn't last very long – all they found were two books and some waste paper!

'Pardon and good evening, monsieurs.'

Although the soldiers were satisfied, the abolitionists' enemies were not. Soon more lies began to circulate.

'Thomas Clarkson has only come to France because the English abolitionists don't want him.'

'Thomas Clarkson is a troublemaker.'

'Thomas Clarkson is an English spy come to destroy us!'

'I think,' Marquis la Fayette said, 'you should move lodgings so that you are closer to my house. That way if a group of actual troublemakers come to your hotel you can call me and I can send some guards to protect you. It would also be a good idea to write a reply to the accusations in the newspaper.'

***

'And what are your views on slavery?' Thomas asked. He was eating dinner with several free black men from the French colony of St. Domingo. After hearing of the French Revolution, they had come to France in the hope of representing their country in the National Assembly alongside their white counterparts.

'The same as yours, friend. We are the descendents of slaves, and until slavery is abolished we will never be granted the same rights as the white citizens. We wish to ask the National Assembly to abolish the slave trade.'

Sadly, this was not to be. Although the French president assured them they had equal rights, each time the day of their hearing at the Assembly came, it was postponed. When this had happened six times, the delegation from St. Domingo grew disheartened.

'We are beginning not to care about the National Assembly any more,' one told Thomas. 'Freedom and equality are our rights. Perhaps we will take them by force.'

'Surely such a thing will bring harm to your country,' Thomas begged. 'If you have patience and wait until this unrest has settled down, the National Assembly will surely listen to you. After all, most of the men there are already on your side.'

'Patience is a most difficult task, friend, but we thank you for your advice.'

'Remember me by this trinket,' said one of the delegates to Thomas before he left, 'I myself will never forget you, because of your deep concern for my Mother Africa.'

It was true that unrest was growing in France. Walking through the streets of Versailles, Thomas saw men gathering at street corners carrying weapons. A few days later the King and Queen of France were taken prisoner and brought to Paris where he was staying. Inside the Anti-Slavery Committee there was also trouble – two out of the six members were revealed to be spies, determined to see the slave trade continued!

Dismayed by the news and tired of waiting for the National Assembly to invite him to speak, Thomas managed to arrange a private meeting with several members.

'Do you think the National Assembly will seek the abolition of slavery at the current time?'

'No,' came the answer again and again, around the table. 'The revolution is more important.'

Two men, however, disagreed. The Marquis la Fayette was still determined to support Thomas. 'If we were to abolish the slave trade immediately, it would make a considerable difference to our fellow human beings who are suffering.'

'I will bring it up in the National Assembly,' promised Count Mirabeau, an ambitious and energetic man.

Regaining hope, Thomas distributed the *Brookes* diagram, copies of his essay, and some illustrations by the Swedish scientists to the members of the National Assembly.

It was the *Brookes* diagram which moved many members in the National Assembly to call upon Thomas in person. The Archbishop of Aix was so horrified he could not speak, and Count Mirabeau was so impressed that he had a wooden model with tiny carved men and women made, to display in his dining room.

Alarmed, many of their enemies wrote letters threatening the Archbishop and offering Mirabeau money if he stepped down. Again the newspapers claimed that Thomas was a spy. All of this reached the King of France who, even though he was ill and a prisoner, asked to see a copy of Thomas' essay and some of his African specimens.

***

'Could you deliver this to Count –'

'– Mirabeau, I know.' said the delivery boy. This was hardly surprising, considering Thomas had been sending him a sixteen to twenty page letter every second day for the past month! He had a lot of information to pass on to this fervent abolitionist.

Sadly, by the time Thomas had to leave France six months later, little had been accomplished. France was just too busy with her internal affairs to discuss the slave trade. Several months later Thomas heard that the St. Domingo delegation had returned home, only to discover that in their absence their fellow black citizens had been persecuted for seeking equal rights. In retaliation the free black population united with the slaves and attacked the slave owners.

St. Domingo, today known as Haiti, erupted into civil war.

***

'Parliament is ready to hear from our witnesses.'

Thomas looked over his list of sixteen names and groaned. While he had been away one witness had died and eight others were at sea. Once again it was time to mount his horse for another journey.

After only three weeks – a record for Thomas – he had three new witnesses. He returned to London only to discover that a very serious question was being debated in the House of Commons: When Africans sold their fellow country men to the white slavers, were they selling people who were already slaves or were they deliberately capturing them to get money from the white slavers?

'It's important,' Thomas explained to a friend in casual conversation, 'because our opponents are arguing that in buying African slaves, they are actually giving them a better life. But we believe that money hungry African leaders are selling their own people into slavery – something they wouldn't do if we weren't buying them!'

'Then you need someone who has witnessed Africans enslaving their own people to testify.'

'Exactly,' said Thomas. 'The problem is, no white man has ever gone on one of the enslaving expeditions.'

'Really?' Thomas' friend replied. 'I met a man a year ago who told me he had. He was talking all about it! I can describe him to you.'

'What's his name?' Thomas asked, suddenly excited. This was exactly what they needed!

'I don't know.'

'Well, where does he live?'

'I'm afraid I don't know that either.'

'Which port was his ship docked at?'

'I don't know!' Thomas' friend threw his hands into the air. 'I'm sorry, I only spoke to him for half an hour at an inn. I was travelling at the time. But he seemed a decent man. I'm sure he'd testify. One thing I do know: He was planning on joining the Navy, on a ship of war.'

Thomas stood up. 'If it is possible to find him,' he said, 'I will do so!'

Sugar, Rum and Dangerous Waters

The problem was, it didn't seem at all possible! Thomas couldn't write a letter because he didn't know the man's name. Yet he had to move quickly, because any day now the abolitionists could be called to present their witnesses.

'You want my permission to search every ship of war in harbour?' Sir Charles Middleton, Comptroller of the Navy, asked. 'For a man whose name you don't know?'

'It's the only way forward I can think of,' replied Thomas. 'If I can't find this man, perhaps I may find another willing to testify.'

'Very well,' agreed Sir Middleton, still as supportive as he had been the night Thomas had promised to end the slave trade. 'I'll give you my written permission.'

The King's docks in Depford were Thomas' first stop. He boarded every ship of war in the harbour and questioned every man on board – but to no success.

From Depford he went to Woolwich, from Woolwich to Chatham, from Chatham to Medway and then on to Sheerness. He made his way through the crews of 160 ships but did not find his witness.

Aware that time was running out, Thomas swung himself back into his saddle. When he arrived at Portsmouth he was confronted by a huge harbour, full of vessels. It would take forever to search! Still, all he could do was board one ship at a time. Thomas settled down to the methodical task. *Please God, let me find him.*

A hundred ships later, and Thomas had still not found the man. It was hard not to feel discouraged. Still, he reminded himself, *I have had many interesting conversations with sailors about the slave trade and gathered other pieces of evidence. Even if I didn't find the sailor I was looking for, it wasn't completely in vain.*

His next and last stop was Plymouth, far away on the opposite coast. On Thomas' first day at the West England dock he boarded forty ships, but didn't find a single sailor who had been on an enslaving expedition in Africa. That night he tossed and turned, his heart beating against his chest as he tried to sleep. *Please God. Tomorrow is my last chance.*

Both hopeful of success and terrified of disappointment, Thomas boarded sixteen ships the next day – none of which carried his witness. When he climbed aboard the seventeenth ship, however, he was met by the object of his quest!

'Yes, I've been on two African expeditions,' said Isaac Parker, a shipkeeper who had also sailed under the explorer Captain Cook. 'I've seen whole villages destroyed and the captives sold to the slavers.'

Thanks to God's gracious provision and Thomas' tenacity, a key witness had been found. It wasn't until much later that Thomas discovered that his brother John had known of Isaac Parker, so perhaps there could have been an easier way to find him. Thomas' search of the 317 ships had taken three weeks – for once the delaying tactics of their opponents in Parliament proved to be a blessing!

***

'Will you bring your shipkeepers and deckcleaners to testify against our admirals?' taunted the slave trade supporters, laughing when Isaac Parker stood up to give his testimony.

'You have examined your admirals and I will examine Isaac Parker,' retorted Wilberforce, rising to his feet. 'And I am certain I will find as much honour, truth and usefulness in Parker's evidence than in all your admirals put together!'

While the battle over the slave trade raged in Parliament, it was also being fought in other areas of society.

'Have you heard William Cowper's new poem?' asked Thomas. While he was always enthusiastic about anything to do with abolition, he particularly enjoyed poetry. 'Listen, it's from the perspective of an African slave:

Forced from home and all its pleasures,
Afric's coast I left forlorn,
To increase a stranger's treasures.

…What are England's rights, I ask,
Me from my delights to sever,
Me to torture, me to task?

'Actually, I've heard it in full,' Thomas' friend interrupted. 'It's been published all over the country and someone has made it into a song. It's very popular.'

A short while later Thomas left on another journey, this time of over 7,000 miles. Hoping to find a hundred witnesses, he returned with only twenty. By now 1,300 pages of evidence had been delivered to the House of Commons, most of it collected on Thomas' travels. Back in London, Thomas, his brother John and their friend William Dickson met with Wilberforce daily to plan their next campaign. By the time Parliament was finally in session, Thomas was so exhausted that in the final week he had to dictate to a clerk from his bed.

Despite this, his new witnesses testified faithfully and clearly, not one of them retracting their statements, even under fierce questioning. Wilberforce's speeches were as eloquent as ever, and many other MPs stood up to declaim the 'monstrous wickedness' of the slave trade. Thomas' brother John joined a committee to establish a free African Colony in Sierra Leone, hoping to provide homes for freed slaves and set up a rival trade route. Thomas supported him and the other evangelical businessmen generously.

Yet after all this, the abolitionists still lost in Parliament that year.

***

'You're wearing yourself out,' said Quaker John Wilkinson. 'You're only a young man, Thomas.'

'I would not change anything,' said Thomas, from his seat beside Wilkinson's fireplace. 'I will be a slave to the slaves as long as God gives me life. I'll be very thankful if I can just live until the end of the next Parliamentary session. Abolition is just around the corner.'

I hope, thought John Wilkinson, looking at the thirty-one-year-old, you'll live much longer than that!

It was 1791 and Thomas was riding once again. He journeyed across England and Wales, even as far as Scotland and the city of Glasgow. His friend William Dickinson visited the other parts of Scotland. They delivered information; promoted abolition meetings; set up new committees; and urged people to sign petitions.

As he made his way from town to town, Thomas slowly became aware of a change taking place. Lord Fox, the MP who had agreed to stand up against slavery at the beginning of the campaign, had recently written a pamphlet which had been widely distributed. In it, Fox explained that refusing to use sugar or rum produced by slaves was one way the population could protest against the slave trade.

This idea, called boycotting, was received with great enthusiasm. Wherever Thomas went he met at least one family who had given up sugar, and often entire villages. Thomas himself refused to eat sugar, and encouraged everyone to read Fox's pamphlet. Women and children who were not allowed to sign petitions were glad to have a way they could stand up against slavery. Wilberforce and the Society were afraid this method would appear too aggressive, but Thomas was enthusiastic.

'Three hundred thousand people,' he estimated, 'have given up the sugar which was bought at the cost of African lives.'

When Thomas arrived in Shropshire the Archdeacon Joseph Plymley offered him a place to stay. 'And I'll come with you tomorrow on your visits,' he said. 'We can leave at 7 a.m.'

Yet when Plymley's sisters, Katherine and Ann, came downstairs the next morning to wish their brother and Thomas a safe journey, they only found Thomas! Waiting in the parlour, he told them he had been up since 6 a.m. and had already written several letters.

'I know it's already seven o'clock,' said Katherine, after a quick check on her brother, 'but Joseph has only just woken.'

Thomas put down his mug of milk. 'I would have begun another letter if I'd known he was going to sleep in.'

'You still have time,' replied Katherine. 'If you fetch your ink and papers, we'll get you a proper writing desk.'

When they met again in the parlour a few minutes later, Thomas had worked out an efficient system. 'If you seal the letters as I write, we'll save even more time,' he said.

Katherine, a faithful abolitionist, agreed.

Despite being a firm believer in punctuality, Thomas' hosts soon discovered that he always had time for children. Sometimes he even allowed himself to fall behind 'schedule' because he was busy answering their questions! He treated them as seriously and with as much respect as he treated every person he met, rich or poor, male or female, black or white. Holding their hands, he listened to their stories and told them funny tales of his own adventures.

'Come again soon!' Children called out when it was time for their six-foot friend to ride off. One young girl even sewed Thomas tiny bags of lavender so his saddle bags would smell pleasant.

In 1792 more petitions were sent into Parliament than ever before: 512, from all over England, Scotland and Wales. In Manchester 20,000 citizens signed, while the city of London presented a petition to Parliament with only minutes to spare, triumphing over the opposition's attempt to prevent it.

Yet despite the enthusiasm of many, Thomas' opponents were backed by something more powerful than signatures: fear.

'You must stop talking about the French Revolution, Clarkson.' Wilberforce told his friend. 'It is making people afraid that we abolitionists want a revolution here in England!'

'But there are plenty who support the oppressed poor in France,' Thomas argued. 'My view is no different to that of many of my friends. Surely I can talk about it with them?'

'It's too dangerous,' Archdeacon Plymley replied. 'You are too well known, and ever since Thomas Paine's book *Rights of Man* was published, the situation here has been unstable.'

'First a revolution in France, then in St. Domingo, next in England.' The rumours came from every direction. 'If we abolish slavery, we will have a revolution! Clarkson and the abolitionists wish to start a civil war!'

Once again, abolition was overturned in Parliament. Instead, the MPs agreed to consider putting a gradual end to the slave trade in the future. This was not a real solution to the problem at all.

***

'You're ill, Thomas.' Archdeacon Plymley said. 'And look at your face!'

Thomas felt the side of his head. It hurt where he pressed. His skin was tender, bruised and swollen from crossing the Bristol Channel in the middle of a storm. Speaking was painful, but he did not want to slow down. Parliament had been adjourned until the following year, but in the next session the slave trade was scheduled to be properly discussed in the House of Lords for the first time. The abolitionists required fresh witnesses.

'I'll come with you,' continued Plymley, 'as far as Oswestry, North Wales.'

When they reached Oswestry, Thomas was determined to press on to Bangor. He waved goodbye to his friend, and waited for the next coach. The idea of sitting inside instead of on a horse was very appealing to Thomas, who had gotten soaking wet in the rain the night before. Yet when the coach arrived it was full.

'Ah well,' Thomas shrugged and climbed up to sit on the top, unprotected from the wind and rain. He nodded to a servant who was also travelling on the outside of the coach, and settled down for the long journey, shivering.

'Your coat is completely wet!' exclaimed the servant. 'Wait a minute.' He rummaged through his master's bags and pulled out his master's cloak. 'My master is inside and doesn't need it.'

'Thank you very much,' said Thomas, pulling his hands out of his pockets and wrapping the cloak unashamedly around him as the coach drove off. The dry fabric made a world of difference.

***

In 1793 France declared war on England. Worried about their own people, Parliament had no energy to spare for the slave trade, and for the first time neither did Thomas Clarkson.

'Ow!' Thomas fell against the wall on his way up the stairs, grazing his shoulder against the wood. The stairs buckled like water beneath his feet and everything spun around. He closed his eyes against the dizziness, but a ringing sound in his ears made his stomach curl.

His symptoms were getting worse.

Gifted with a very good memory, over the past few months Thomas had found himself unable to remember facts and details. It was a struggle to concentrate and if he spoke or wrote for over half an hour at a time he began sweating and had to stop from sheer exhaustion.

At last he was realising that abolition might not happen for many years. If he wore himself out now he might not live long enough to see it! Thomas picked up his pen and with great sadness began to write a letter to the Abolition Society and his close friends.

'My constant travel and lack of sleep, the disappointments and anxiety, the awful stories I hear all day long, are beginning to ruin my health. I am not sure whether I should keep going.'

His friends were very sympathetic and urged him to rest and recover. Homes in the country were opened to him and financial assistance was also offered, because Thomas had spent almost all his inheritance supporting abolition and the Sierra Leone Company.

When Thomas arrived in Cumbria at the forty acre farm belonging to his friend John Wilkinson, he was a broken man. Life with the Quaker and his two sisters however, proved to be exactly what Thomas needed. Wilkinson was a farmer, poet and keen reader. While staying with him, Thomas breakfasted at 7 a.m. and went to bed at 9 p.m. He took the medicine he had been prescribed, cast off his dark clerical robes, and spent the days working in the field, grooming his horse and enjoying the beautiful scenery.

'I've bought some land near Ullswater Lake,' said Thomas, a short while later. 'The Lake District is striking and I am planning on building a house. From the windows I will be able to see the towering blue peak of Mount Helvellyn. You should see it in the evening, it's breathtaking.'

Archdeacon Plymley stared at his excited friend. Thomas had not said one word about abolition since his arrival – and normally he spoke of nothing else!

'I can help you draw up the plan for the house,' Katherine Plymley offered, glad to see Thomas looking so much healthier.

'And I can give you drawing lessons,' the Archdeacon added, 'so that you can send us pictures of the beautiful area you are describing.'

Thomas sat at a table strewn with papers. This was not unusual, but the contents of these pages were! Instead of letters about slavery, they were filled with sketches of horses and dogs. He would give them as gifts to the children after lunch, Thomas decided, as he wrote the Archdeacon's rules of perspective in his drawing notebook.

'What trees and bushes will you plant?' Katherine asked her friend as they strolled around the gardens that afternoon.

Thomas watched the sun dancing through the lush green trees near the path. 'Cheerful ones,' he said.

While Thomas had certainly fallen in love with the Lake District, he also fell in love with someone else during this time – a woman by the name of Catherine Buck.

A Good Man's Happiness

Catherine Buck was thirteen years younger than Thomas, and they first met in her abolitionist uncle's parlour. Thomas had shown the household the contents of his famous crate, and Catherine had been moved by the plight of the African slaves.

Catherine was a well-read, spirited woman. While Thomas stayed with her uncle she helped him make copies of sheets of evidence and questions for MPs. Like Thomas, she had initially been supportive of the French Revolution. Sadly, she does not appear to have been a Christian when they married in 1796, although evidence suggests she came to follow God later on.

Thomas, now thirty-five years old, felt it was the perfect time to settle down at last. The fear of revolution meant that it was illegal to hold meetings of more than fifty people. The Society for Abolition was no longer holding any meetings. Wilberforce's bill to abolish the slave trade by 1797 – a year later than originally promised – had failed in Parliament because a dozen abolitionist voters were out attending an opera.

To have all our efforts wasted over four votes, thought Thomas, *is discouraging and frustrating! Still, there is nothing I can do but turn the abolition cause over to God for the time being, and trust in his goodness and justice.*

A year later Wilberforce also married.

The passion Thomas had shown in pursuing abolition, he now turned to his new life in the country.

'He sums up his evidence for and against his hen-pens and goose-house with as much detail and precision as he summed up the evidence of the slave trade!' the Archdeacon Plymley said. 'He will make a very good farmer, because it will be a work of both body and mind.'

'Even so,' Plymley's sister replied, 'I don't expect he will remain retired for very long. He was born to serve mankind in the public sphere.'

Thomas soon found, however, that his new 'private' life kept him just as busy as politics! In October, Catherine gave birth to a baby boy, and they called him Thomas. Once he was three years old, his mother began to teach him the alphabet while she churned butter, planted potatoes, and studied botany!

***

'Excuse me,' said Thomas, as soon as the door opened. 'Do you have any strange cows in your fields?'

The farmer stared. 'I'm not sure, have you lost some?'

'No, I'm asking for my neighbour,' Thomas explained. 'He's a poor man, and he's lost his cows.'

'Try the next house.'

Thomas continued his door-knocking, visiting every farm in the area until he found the cows. Like always, tales of suffering moved him deeply, and he regularly visited and helped ten of the poorer families in the neighbourhood, just like his father before him had done. He was also genuinely interested in their lives and the way they lived because he knew he had a lot to learn about country living.

'In the country,' Thomas wrote, 'anyone can be pleased. But the spiritual man experiences a higher joy, because he converses with God in his works. In the country the Christian finds himself grateful for God's goodness, acknowledges his wisdom, and admires his power.'

It was not always easy living in the country, particularly when a bitter winter meant a poor harvest, but Thomas bore these hardships as patiently as he had borne the cold and the wet during his horseback journeys. It helped that he and Catherine had made some good friends.

'I never saw so sweet a sight,' said Samuel Coleridge, pointing at Ullswater Lake. William Wordsworth and his sister Dorothy agreed.

The poets and the Clarksons soon became known as the 'Wordsworth Circle,' sharing houses, lives and many, many letters, even when they no longer lived close by. When Wordsworth married his wife Mary, they named their two children Catherine and Thomas. Although young Thomas had not been named after Thomas Clarkson, Catherine had been named after Catherine Clarkson, and the Wordsworths wrote to say they would think of both of them when they looked at their children!

'Tom,' Coleridge asked one day, 'do you ever worry about where your soul will end up after death?'

'How can I?' asked Thomas, watching as the sun set over the lake. 'Any spare time I have goes to thinking about the slaves in Barbados!' Thomas knew that the God who created the seasons and brought forth the harvest each year was quite capable of bringing the souls who trusted him safely Home. In the meantime, God had given Thomas work to do on earth.

Later Thomas would exchange letters with the often melancholy poet about the nature of God and the human soul. Although Coleridge did not share Thomas' Christian beliefs, he admired his steadfastness. 'Thomas Clarkson is a moral steam engine,' he would tell people. 'He is like a giant with one idea.' It was certainly true that even as Thomas embraced farming wholeheartedly, he had not forgotten about the slave trade.

'It makes him very distressed to talk about it,' one visitor wrote, 'but when he does, he distresses everyone around him.' It seemed that no one could go away unmoved after hearing Thomas talk about the enslaved Africans. Even in his 'retirement' Thomas was still enlisting supporters!

***

All too soon the Clarksons' idyllic life was shattered.

'Ow! Oh dear. Ow.' Catherine clutched her stomach.

'What is it?' Thomas asked, hurrying over. 'What's wrong?'

'Such sharp pains ...' Catherine's suffering only got worse, and when the local doctors had no remedy left to offer, she travelled to Bristol to see Thomas Beddoes, whom some called the best doctor in England.

'You must leave the Lake District,' he told her, 'it is far too cold there.'

With Catherine staying at her family's house, it was up to Thomas to put everything in order at their beloved home before finding a buyer. As he did, he filled his free time with his latest project.

'I'm writing a book on the Quakers,' he told his Quaker friend Wilkinson. 'So few people really understand your way of life and your thoughts on spiritual matters. As a result you are not taken seriously. I think my three volumes may do some good.' As always, Thomas felt the need to stand up for those who were ignored by society.

'What if he writes cruel things about us?' worried some of the Quakers. 'Many people spread rumours about us which are not true at all.'

'He is trying to make it as accurate as possible,' Wilkinson reassured his friends. 'He gives each volume to me to check after he has finished. We should try and help him, because he's doing this out of a love for truth, a desire to grant us justice, and a wish to enrich mankind.'

Catherine also began to read about the Quakers, and soon her friends noticed a change in her thinking. 'She has become a believer,' one said.

'My ever dear friend,' wrote Dorothy Wordsworth to Catherine, 'may God restore you to health and may you come back to us soon.'

***

'Abolition hovers on the horizon.'

'Now Ireland and England have united, there are one hundred new Irish Members of Parliament, most of whom are pro-abolition.'

'There is no longer any fear of an English Revolution, not now that everyone's seen how France has turned out under Napoleon!'

Thomas gazed around the table at his fellow abolitionists. It was 1804 and after seven years the Society had resumed its activity. There were several new faces, many of them Wilberforce's friends. Thomas had come out of retirement, sensing the time was ripe for abolition, and he saw now that it had been a good decision.

That year Wilberforce's bill was overturned in Parliament, as it had been every year he had presented it, but at least it went as far as the House of Lords. When the following year brought another failure, Wilberforce and Thomas refused to be discouraged.

'It was an accident,' said Thomas.

'We only lost because the MPs were so certain abolition would win, that they left without voting!' agreed Wilberforce. 'We won't have any problems winning next year.'

'If that's true, this will be my last journey,' said Thomas, as he mounted his horse once more. It was also his first journey as a married man, and so it looked a little bit different.

'It's a miracle from God you are still with me,' he told Catherine, when she was well enough to join him on part of his travels.

'I know I joked about dying cheerfully,' she replied, 'but I am very glad to be alive!'

At Shropshire the couple stayed with Archdeacon Plymley and his sister Katherine. There, Thomas pushed his wife around the garden in her wheelchair, while the rest of the household read his manuscript on the Quakers and gave him feedback.

'Unusually interesting,' said Katherine Plymley. Mostly likely she had expected that reading about the Quakers would be as dull as their dark clothes!

While in Shropshire, Thomas joined the Archdeacon's catechism class, and both he and Catherine enjoyed attending family prayers and Sunday church with their friends. Before too long, however, Thomas was on the road again.

As he headed towards Scotland, Thomas reflected on yet another difference. In the past he had spent all his energy hunting down witnesses. Now, however, he found that a lot of his time was occupied in reviving local abolition committees and encouraging old supporters. He was also busy sharing information and equipping a new, younger generation of abolitionists. The times had certainly changed, and he was now building on the foundation he and the Society had laid so many years before.

Thomas returned to London at last, satisfied for the first time with what he had achieved on one of his journeys – only to be met with sad news.

'Prime Minister William Pitt has died.'

Thomas mourned the loss of the energetic and clever forty-six-year-old who had supported abolition in Parliament for so long. Pitt's death also raised some serious questions: What if the next Prime Minister was pro-slavery? Would this cause trouble in Parliament? But by God's grace, Lord Grenville came into power, supported by Charles Fox. Both men were loyal abolitionists: the fight to end the slave trade would continue.

'We have heard so much evil about the slave trade that cruelty has become familiar to us!' argued Lord Grenville. 'But try to think once more of the lives of these men and women who have no rest, no hope, no peace.'

To Thomas' joy, a bill was passed in 1806 to abolish the part of the slave trade which brought slaves to

Britain's captured colonies. Surely this was a sign that the abolition of the entire slave trade would soon be accomplished.

After this, Lord Fox stood up. 'I want to ask Parliament to affirm in a bill that the African slave trade is contrary to the principles of justice, humanity and policy. I have sat in this House for forty years, and if seeing this statement passed in Parliament is all I do, my life will not have been lived in vain.'

This bill too was passed! It was the first condemnation of slavery in the entire nineteen-year campaign. Two smaller bills designed to hinder the slave trade were also met with success. Change was in the air, Thomas was certain.

Shortly afterwards, fifty-six-year-old Lord Fox also died. On his deathbed he spoke to those around him, saying: 'I wish to see peace with Europe and the slave trade abolished, but out of the two I'd prefer abolition, because England at least has some hope of protection from their enemies, but the African people have none.'

'Lord Fox,' Thomas said, 'saw abolition as the greatest earthly blessing a government could ever give.'

***

'Here's my list of MPs to lobby about the slave trade,' said Thomas, beginning to prepare for the new Parliamentary term. It was 1807.

Wilberforce looked at the page. 'A terrific list of doubtfuls! I'm not sure how many of them will agree to support us.' He laughed. 'Still, God can change men's hearts, and I think we may yet win!'

When the day for the debate came, MPs fought for a chance to speak ... against the slave trade! Man after man stood up, proof that God, using Thomas' evidence and Wilberforce's speeches, had indeed changed many hearts. Thomas stared as men who had been strong opponents to slavery left the room because they felt unable to continue in their beliefs. Still others, convicted by all they had heard and seen, gladly voted against slavery.

Shortly after midnight on 24th February, the African slave trade was abolished! Two hundred and eighty-three MPs voted for abolition, and only sixteen opposed the bill. Thomas suspected that it was the largest majority the House had ever seen! Twenty-two years ago he had written an essay and surrendered it to God, and today he knew that because of it, the world would never be the same.

In Parliament, Wilberforce was in tears. Thomas spent the rest of the day writing letters to all the abolition supporters:

'Our efforts were blessed by God last night, and I have no words to express the joy I feel. My heart is full of gratitude to the Parent of all Mercies, that he has been pleased to offer a portion of my life to my fellow oppressed creatures.'

Unfortunately the Parliamentary Bill still had to receive royal consent.

'Prime Minister Grenville has been dismissed by the King. He has to leave Parliament by 11.30 a.m., 25th March. If the King doesn't agree to the abolition bill by then, all will be lost!'

Thomas paced the room and throughout England abolitionists waited and prayed.

Just in time, with the midday sun blazing over the houses of Parliament, the royal assent came through and Grenville left the House, content in the knowledge that it was his government which had ended the slave trade.

The country rejoiced and people everywhere praised God; the work of the abolitionists; and in particular, Thomas Clarkson and William Wilberforce. Wordsworth even wrote a sonnet about his friend:

Clarkson! It was an obstinate hill to climb:
How toilsome, nay, how dire, it was.
... [But] see the palm is won, and by all nations shall be worn!
The blood-stained writing is forever torn,
and thou henceforth will have a good man's calm,
a great man's happiness; your zeal shall find
repose at length, firm friend of humankind!

The Fight Continues

'Thomas, you have to write a book about all that's happened.'

'I don't want to write a book about myself!' Thomas protested, uncomfortable with the fact that he had somehow become a hero. His dedication and his tireless travel throughout the kingdom, despite so many dangers, had earned him much respect in the eyes of many.

'But no one knows as much as you about the abolition, particularly about all the work which happened outside of Parliament.'

At last Thomas agreed. Never good at keeping his writing short, his work, *The History of the Abolition of the African Slave Trade*, was published in two large volumes. It was a commercial success.

'I've dedicated it to Pitt and Fox.' Thomas told his wife.

'The final sentence is very moving,' said Catherine. 'Reader,' she read, 'if you feel grateful for the abolition, retire into your room and pour out your thanksgivings to the Almighty, because this is his unspeakable act of mercy.'

Thomas and family were now living in Bury St. Edmunds, Catherine's childhood home. Here Thomas found time to help open a school for poor children; found a branch of the British and Foreign Bible Society; fight against capital punishment; and establish a peace society with his brother John. He also wrote and published an essay promoting pacifism, pointing out that war can never be justified, and there is no such thing as a 'holy war' for Christians today – only to find himself attacked by many evangelicals because his writing was too 'subversive'. But despite these other interests, his dealings with slavery were not yet over.

'Now the trading of slaves is illegal,' said a member of the Society, 'we must make sure traders obey the new law. If they do, the practice of slavery will die out too.'

With this new aim in mind, the Society for Abolition became the African Institution.

* * *

'I can't believe it!' exclaimed Thomas. 'How could the British Government sign a treaty allowing France to continue trading slaves for five more years?'

'It is the same as signing a death warrant for thousands of Africans,' agreed Wilberforce. 'Something must be done.'

Although the slave trade was abolished in Britain, Thomas didn't feel he could rest.

'My dearest love,' he wrote to Catherine, 'The Congress of Vienna is our next chance to influence the European leaders. If we do nothing, the European slave trade may continue for another twenty or thirty years.'

Once again, Thomas was surrounded by piles of paper. He had set up headquarters at the New London Tavern, and posted 2,000 letters to encourage people to petition Parliament and change the wording of the treaty. He also had several of his anti-slavery booklets nicely bound and sent to the King of Prussia and the Tsar of Russia.

The Tsar of Russia was interested in abolition, and grateful to receive Thomas' books. When he read one on his circuitous trip to Vienna he told his courtiers that the reports of slavery it contained made him sicker than his rough English Channel crossing.

Catherine and their son joined Thomas in London as he worked. Soon, however, Thomas had a new plan.

'I want to be in Vienna when the European powers meet,' he told a shocked Wilberforce, and began at once to prepare a speech to the heads of state:

'You yourselves have been great sufferers… if you sign to abolish the slave trade from the entire world, you are showing your gratitude to God for the blessings you have received.'

'You should not go,' Wilberforce argued. 'If the official British representative fails to convince France, you could be blamed and since you are director of the African Institution, it would reflect badly on the organisation.'

In the parlour of Wilberforce's London home, Thomas sighed. He thought his friend was being far too cautious. The slave trade must be stopped! 'Very well,' he said. 'I won't go to Vienna, but for no other reason than because you are my friend and it is your wish.'

'Thank you,' said Wilberforce, much relieved.

'I would still like to go to Paris, at least, and visit my French abolitionist friends,' Thomas said.

He and Catherine crossed the Channel, and while she saw the sights, he toiled for fourteen hours a day alongside the French abolitionists.

'My dear Clarkson,' said one French aristocrat, 'you shouldn't spend so much time with some of these people, they are not very well-bred.'

'I know only two classes of people – the friends of Africa and the enemies of Africa,' replied Thomas, 'And all the friends of Africa are equal in my eyes.'

While in France, the Duke of Wellington contacted Thomas. 'The French king cannot now do anything against the voice of the people. In order to see the slave trade destroyed in France, we must change the voice of the people.'

Luckily, Thomas knew just what to do!

'Excuse me, do you have a copy of my booklet? It is called *The Impolicy of the Slave Trade*.' Thomas asked this in every bookshop he could find. 'It was printed here in France twenty-five years ago.'

Finally one bookshop owner found a copy. 'Here, Monsieur Clarkson! Here!'

Thomas rushed the booklet to the publishers, where it was cleared to print in a record twelve hours, and distributed across France. All too soon, however, it was time for him to return to Britain.

Meanwhile, in Vienna, the European leaders decided they were unable to agree to worldwide abolition.

***

'Ooh, how beautiful France looks from here!' Thomas' nineteen-year-old son exclaimed as their boat neared Calais. After practising his French for several months, Thomas had decided to return to Paris, with the goal of speaking in person with the visiting Russian Tsar Alexander I. This time Catherine stayed at home.

It was just as well. Paris shimmered in the Summer heat, and Thomas and his son slept with their windows open every night as they waited for an audience with the Tsar. At last Thomas received an invitation, and suddenly nervous, was ushered into Alexander I's rooms.

'Where should I stand? What should I say?' Thomas wiped his damp palms. *Please help me, God. This is your work.*

The imposing door opened at last to reveal the Tsar himself, standing for his guest! Alexander I took Thomas by the hand and led him into the room.

'Thank you so much for visiting me, I have long wished to meet you,' the Tsar said in such a friendly and honest way that Thomas at once felt relieved. 'Your writings have greatly impacted me. When I saw the diagram of the *Brookes* slave ship, I knew that unless I did my best to abolish slavery, I would be unworthy of the power God has given me as emperor of Russia.'

The two men spoke for over an hour. Thomas soon found that the rumours about the Tsar's faith and compassion were true. It was a pity Thomas could not examine the Emperor's trousers, which were said to be worn at the knee from all the time he spent praying!

'Are you a Quaker?' asked Alexander I.

Thomas paused. He had long since dropped the title 'Reverend', and was in fact disgusted with many of the Church of England clergymen who took the office only to earn money, spending their days drinking and hunting. 'Not in name, but I agree with almost all of their thoughts,' he answered. 'They have been my fellow labourers in the great cause of abolition, and the more I know them, the more I love them.'

Thomas, always straightforward, then told the Tsar that Russia could be even more great if he introduced a national system of education guided by Christian principles. When the time came to say goodbye, the Tsar said, 'If I can at any time be useful to the cause of the poor Africans, you may always have my services by writing me a letter.'

It was Thomas, however, who would receive a letter that same year, this time from another sovereign: the King of Haiti. Henry I, the son of a slave himself, wrote to Thomas thanking him for his work in destroying the slave trade. He wished to do what was best for his country, and asked Thomas' help in establishing an education system. Thomas wrote back, offering to put him in touch with some Quakers who were planning on visiting the West Indies. 'Whenever you see a Quaker, you see a friend of the distressed,' he said.

Their letters continued, Thomas genuinely excited for the King's ambitious plans for his country. When the 1818 European Congress in France was announced, Thomas was determined to attend, hoping to win support for Haiti as well as international abolition. This time Wilberforce didn't stop him.

'Thomas Clarkson seems formed by God for this purpose,' he told a friend. 'We may depend on his serious dedication and, as he is regarded as half-Quaker, he may do eccentric things with less offense than you or I could!'

For this trip Thomas took his nephew, and while waiting for an interview with Alexander I, showed him the sights.

'Uncle, look at his coat!'

Thomas, after a quick glance at Lord Castlereagh's diamond-encrusted coat, turned away. He hated taxes, and despised the fact that the poor English people were paying for needless extravagance. One evening Thomas' banker invited them to a dinner which lasted three-and-a-half hours, and Thomas was appalled. 'I calculated that the servants would have had to wash 700 plates,' he wrote to Catherine, 'All was splendid and luxurious, and I was never so tired of anything in my life!'

Again the European Congress failed to promote international abolition, and when it congregated four years later, the result was the same. Thomas and Wilberforce had both written appeals to the rulers without success.

Meanwhile Thomas received some terrible news.

'There's been an uprising in Haiti. King Henry I is dead and his wife and daughters have fled. They have nowhere to stay.'

'They can stay with us,' Thomas and Catherine offered, 'at Playford Hall.'

The three ladies came to stay with the Clarksons, something which caused quite a stir in high society, even among the abolitionists. Thomas was unperturbed. 'Of course their skin is black, just like ink,' he said when asked, 'and a more delightful family never entered anyone's house.'

When the queen and the princesses could find no other accommodation after several weeks, Thomas agreed to take them on as paying guests.

'Although make sure you make it clear that they are paying,' he told the man who arranged it. 'I don't want to receive credit for being generous where I am not!'

The Clarksons loved and admired their Haitian guests, who had been spared in the rebellion because they were so well known for their good deeds to the oppressed. The three women loved the Clarksons in return.

'See the beautiful silk handkerchiefs they sewed me as a gift!' Thomas said, rummaging in his pocket. 'The two princesses are the most charming young ladies, and full of good sense.' From Thomas, who believed firmly that women should receive an education and not simply exist to amuse society like so many believed, this was high praise indeed.

'Goodbye!' It was with sad hearts that Thomas and Catherine waved their friends off. The three Haitians had found they could no longer tolerate the cold British weather, and decided to relocate to Italy. Neither husband nor wife had time to grieve, however. They both spent many hours looking after their tenants and other poor families. Catherine was heavily involved in running their farm, and Thomas was just beginning a new campaign.

It was time for the abolition of slavery itself, and yet another new society. Wilberforce and Thomas sat on the committee alongside many young and energetic abolitionists, and it was given the rather lengthy name of the Society for Mitigating and Gradually Abolishing the State of Slavery throughout the British Dominions. Once more Thomas picked up his pen to write against slavery. He also got back on his horse.

'It is everyone's opinion, in all England and Wales, that slavery will soon fall!' Thomas rejoiced to his wife on his return. He had travelled over 10,000 miles on two journeys of eight and five months. At sixty-four years of age, he looked older than he was.

'But so cheerful and sociable!' people commented.

'He doesn't mind laughing at himself,' one lady said, 'and he says the funniest things with a straight face, just to make others laugh.'

Thomas bent his neck until his nose was practically smudging his writing. He was beginning to have a hard time seeing. 'If I work hard today,' he told a member of the Society, 'I shall finish the 312 letters I am writing to our correspondents about organising petitions.'

***

'Order, order!' Thomas looked at the 2,000 people crowded into the hall for the anti-slavery rally. How different this was to all those years ago, when only twelve men had sat around a table and pledged to abolish slavery. What a wonderful thing God had accomplished. 'I want to call upon Mr. Wilberforce to chair this meeting as the great leader of our cause.'

William Wilberforce's health was failing, and he came onto the stage slowly. 'No one more dear to me could have called me up,' he said. 'Thomas Clarkson is my valued friend and fellow labourer. He began before me, and we have spent many happy days working towards abolition.'

Three years later in 1833, after the establishment of 1,300 anti-slavery Society branches and 5,484 petitions to Parliament, slavery itself was finally abolished.

'Slavery is no more!' Thomas was overjoyed. 'I am so thankful to have lived long enough to see this day. Our eyes have seen a great salvation,' he said, quoting Luke 2:30, '... and we have had a hand in it too!'

***

'Thomas?' Catherine found her husband in the parlour. 'I have something to tell you. It's bad news. William Wilberforce is dead.'

Thomas stared for a moment, and then turned and rushed into his study. He locked the door and then burst into tears. For a long time Catherine heard him wailing through the wooden partition.

'... every good wish for you and yours, in time and for eternity, my dear old friend.' Thomas remembered Wilberforce's last letter to him and wept some more. It was as though a gaping hole had been torn open in his chest. Out of the original Society only he and the printer Richard Phillips were left. Not only so, but Thomas was now completely blind, unable to read his own writing. For someone who had spent his entire life reading and writing, this was a hard blow indeed.

Thomas clung to his Saviour. 'Although I may be destined to live in a world where all earthly objects are invisible to me,' he told a friend, 'you are not to bemoan my situation – it may be good for me, good for my eternal interests, and better than I could have designed for myself.'

Every evening before bed Catherine read the Bible to him for an hour, taking notes on his behalf. After one such evening, they also read the newspaper which contained a report about a recent murder. The next morning Thomas had a very strange story to tell.

'I dreamt I was dead,' he told Catherine at breakfast, 'and I was looking at my toes to check to see if they'd laid me out straight on the bed. Then an angel appeared and told me God had sent him to give me a sword, because some men were coming to steal my body. When they came I was to cut their ears off – so I did!' For the next few days every time Catherine and Thomas looked at each other they burst out laughing, remembering his dream!

***

'Good morning, Mr. Clarkson.'

Thomas turned his head towards the voice. 'Sara?' he asked, recognising the voice of his old friend, and the sister of Mary Wordsworth.

'Yes, I've come to stay for a while!'

'Surely you are a gift from God,' said Thomas. 'I've worn poor Catherine out by asking her to write notes for me. Would you sit beside me and copy out twenty pages?'

Because it was Thomas, the twenty pages ended up being closer to thirty! Luckily for Sara, who jokingly described Thomas as a modern day 'Blind Bartimaeus,' another gift soon came Thomas' way.

Come, Come my Beloved

'Cataract surgery? What does that involve?' Thomas tried to keep his excitement down. Was it possible he would soon see again?

In 1834, an operation lasting fifty-nine seconds wonderfully restored sight to Thomas' right eye. A relatively new procedure, it only involved removing the clouded lens, but still proved remarkably effective.

One of his first letters after the surgery was a detailed description of his miracle to a friend, and the following Sunday Thomas spoke to his vicar. 'You must give a public thanks to God in my name, for his mercy, his great mercy, in the partial restoration of my sight.'

Thomas threw himself back into his theological studies. 'In Oxford many people have been claiming that we can know God without the Bible, through our own reasoning or through nature alone. I am going to write a book to prove that we need God's written revelation for salvation.'

'No one is buying religious works at the moment,' a bookseller warned him. 'It might not be very popular.'

'That doesn't matter,' Thomas replied. 'I have written my book so that it might be useful for others, not to gain money for myself.'

His next book was about baptism, arguing that water alone could not bring salvation, but faith in Jesus had to accompany it.

Thomas and Catherine's friend Sara died from a fever before the book she had helped copy was published. Coleridge had died the year before, and their other close friend Mary Lamb six months later. It was a sad time for the Clarkson family.

Then, in 1837, Thomas received some even more devastating news. His forty-year-old son had been killed in a carriage accident.

'My son has been taken from me.' Thomas wrote to a friend, still numb with shock. Both Catherine and he mourned deeply and opened their home to their son's widow and little boy.

'May the Almighty God support you,' Wordsworth wrote to Catherine, 'and your husband, through this and all the trials that await the remainder of your days ...'

Before long, Thomas found himself in another situation where he desperately needed God's strength.

'They've attacked you viciously!' said Catherine, storming across the parlour. 'The biography the Wilberforce sons have written of their father is full of lies about you from beginning to end.'

Thomas looked down at the book in his hands, and closed his eyes. He had read many painful things in his life, but to read such an awful book by the sons of his dead friend William Wilberforce was heartbreaking.

'They've written such terrible things to try and give their father all the glory,' Catherine continued. 'They dare claim that you have tried to steal all the honour for yourself!'

Thomas, genuinely shocked, wrote to the two sons. He told them that he had never tried to claim honour for himself, on the contrary many pages of his published *History* listed the names of everyone he could remember who had fought for abolition, and gave much praise to God.

'We must wait,' Catherine decided, once her indignation had died down. 'Perhaps after all this, the mountain will only bring forth a little mouse.'

Unfortunately it proved to be a very big mouse indeed! The two Wilberforce sons published their five volume work, *The Life of William Wilberforce*, in 1838 without clearing Thomas' name. The reading public were indignant.

'Everyone of common sense knows that the merit was Clarkson's and not Wilberforce's,' one newspaper wrote.

'It would be a crime if we left Thomas Clarkson, a dying lion, unprotected while these young things kick him!' declared another supporter.

Even a friend of the Wilberforces admitted, 'it truly gives me heartache to imagine the pain which the old man, Thomas Clarkson, will have to endure.'

In quick succession, Thomas' own *History of the Abolition* was republished; an artist was commissioned to paint his portrait; Thomas Taylor began to write a biographical sketch of his life; and a marble bust of his head was ordered by the City of London!

At the same time, Thomas, now eighty years old and very frail, began to write a book on the life of William Wilberforce to correct the Wilberforce sons' errors. Like always he believed that the truth deserved to be heard, although he wished very much that he did not need to write such a book!

'It's the only writing project which has given me no satisfaction,' he said, 'but only unmingled pain.'

In response, the sons of Wilberforce, who were archdeacons and bishops in the Church of England, threatened to write worse things about Thomas if he published anything which could harm them. Meanwhile, they refused to return letters Thomas had given them at the very beginning when they'd asked for his help with their biography.

Shortly afterwards Thomas was awarded with the freedom of the City of London as a 'grateful testimony' to the man 'who originated and lived to witness the great struggle for the deliverance of the enslaved African.'

Thomas, in his own book, only ever corrected the blatant errors and never complained when he was 'written out' or left unacknowledged for the work he had done. He saw abolition as God's work which he and

Wilberforce and the other Society members had been graciously given to do, working together as different members of one body – something he had said many times before.

It wasn't until 1844 that the two sons attempted an apology, and they never made it public. Nevertheless, Thomas sent the two men a gracious letter of forgiveness, explaining that he understood how difficult it can be to admit to error, and that he did not wish to be at odds with the children of the dear, departed friend whom he had loved and revered.

Sadly, the damage to Thomas' name and contribution had been done, and even today few have heard of his story, while the name of William Wilberforce has achieved worldwide renown.

Thomas, characteristically, burnt his letters and personal papers with efficient regularity. Even if his wife or friends had wished to write a memoir on his behalf, there was no material with which to do so! In the years since his death only two biographies have been written, and they are both out of print.

***

'I long very much to be well again,' Thomas said at eighty-five years old, crippled by arthritis, his eyesight again failing. 'I cannot endure an idle life.'

He was still vice-president of what was now the British and Foreign Anti-Slavery Society, and spent as much time as he could each day writing to friends and abolitionists across the globe, particularly North America. He created a petition and wrote many letters to Parliament seeking to abolish apprenticeships of former slaves, as well as the importation of cheap workers from India.

'Such practices are simply a new form of slavery,' he pointed out.

'What shall we read tonight?' Catherine asked, as the clock in Playford Hall struck 7 p.m. 'A sermon? That history on West Africa? Or the latest book on Ancient Egypt, the one you love so much?'

'Could you read that book given to me by the Wesleyan Missionary Society?' Thomas asked, closing his eyes and folding his aching, arthritic fingers across his chest. 'I promised to write a review on it.'

'And after that,' Catherine continued, 'I'd better cut a few more locks of your hair. We've received more letters begging for them.' The reality was, Thomas had become such a hero that locks of his now-grey hair were prized treasures!

'Soon you won't have any left!' remarked a friend.

Thomas, his young grandson on his knees, shrugged. 'Never mind, shear away!' He had as little concern for outward fashion as ever!

***

'I stand before you as a humble individual, under God. I am now unhappily the only surviving member of the 1787 Abolition Society,' Thomas Clarkson told the crowd. 'Yet my heart beats as warmly for this cause now, as it did when I was twenty-four. If I had another life given me to live, I would devote it to the same object.'

The Anti-Slavery General Convention was being held in London that year. In front of Thomas stood 5,000 delegates from all across the world, including Canada, France, the U.S.A., the West Indies, Haiti, Spain, Switzerland and Sierra Leone. Beside him stood his nine-year-old grandson, whom Thomas had insisted on bringing. It was his birthday that day.

'You must take courage,' Thomas told the crowd, as he spoke of the types of slavery which still existed. In his passion he began to shed tears. 'Do not be dismayed, go on, persevere to the last,' he urged. 'Ahead of us lies the task of removing slavery from the whole world.'

As soon as he finished the crowd erupted, clapping, shouting, and shaking their handkerchiefs and hats for several minutes. The next Sunday, Thomas Clarkson sent a note asking if he and his daughter-in-law could visit the delegates to personally thank the American women who had come, for their work and sacrifice. This was after the British had first refused the women entry into the convention, and then only allowed them to sit removed from the rest of the male attendees.

A few months later, Thomas was woken in the middle of the night. This time his dream was no laughing matter. 'I heard a voice,' he told Catherine the next morning, 'It said, 'you have not done all your work. There is America!' And I remembered that I'd promised to write a pamphlet for the American abolitionists.'

So Thomas pulled out his writing materials once again, with the help of his wife and other volunteer scribes. 'I can't believe that so many people are still arguing that slavery is biblical!' he exclaimed. 'It seems ridiculous that I, an old man, should have to write to refute their arguments.'

But write Thomas did, right until the end. Each tract, he declared, would be his last. Then in September 1846, he became too weak to leave his bed. He was eighty-six. In the corner of his room sat his father's heavy, old lantern. Thomas, in his love for God and lifelong compassion for the poor and oppressed, had certainly followed in his father's footsteps.

'I'm not afraid to die,' he murmured to his wife, 'but it hurts to think of leaving you and the others.'

'Are you in pain?'

'I am very happy,' Thomas assured her. 'I spend all my time praying and I don't wish to do anything else. I wonder what my last thoughts will be?'

'I hope, my dear, of your God and Saviour.' Catherine replied. She was right. At 4 o'clock in the morning of 26th September, 1846, Thomas woke up and raised his hands together. He looked up towards heaven.

'Come, come, come my Beloved,' Thomas begged, and then he went to be with his Lord.

While Thomas' funeral and burial were extremely simple, as he had requested, the words of those he left behind are ample evidence of a life lived humbly for God and man. From Haiti a letter came with the following eulogy:

> The mission of the venerable Thomas Clarkson was marked [by Providence] and that religious man has fulfilled it with all the fidelity and all the zeal of an apostle.
>
> His perseverance, his virtues, have found their reward, even in this world ... rendering glory to his Creator who had designed him to be an instrument of good fortune ...
>
> White and black, we work together... each in the circle which he is given to follow, since the cause of liberty is the cause of God himself.

Thomas Clarkson
Timeline

1760   Thomas Clarkson is born at Wisbech, 28 March.

1766   Thomas' father dies, leaving behind his wife and three children.

1785   Thomas wins essay competition, arguing that no man has the right to make another captive against their will.

1786   Thomas publishes his essay *An Essay on the Slavery and Commerce of the Human Species, particularly the African*.

1787   Thomas pledges his life to abolition; the Society for the Abolition of the Slave Trade is formed; William Wilberforce agrees to bring the matter before Parliament; Thomas leaves on the first of many evidence-collecting journeys.

1788   Wilberforce is ill. William Pitt introduces the matter to Parliament. The Dolben Act is passed, regulating the number of slaves ships can carry.

1789   Thomas visits France after the revolution to advocate for abolition.

1791   The Sierra Leone Company is formed to establish the first African settlement not fueled by slavery. Thomas is a director.

1792   Sugar boycotts begin. A record 512 petitions are sent into Parliament.

1793 War with France begins. Thomas falls ill.

1796 Thomas marries Catherine Buck and retires to the Lake District. They have a son and become friends with the Wordsworths, the Lambs and Coleridge.

1804 Abolition revives.

1806 Thomas publishes his *Portraiture of Quakerism*.

1807 An Act for the Abolition of the Slave Trade is passed successfully.

1808 Thomas publishes his *History of the Abolition of the Slave Trade*.

1814 Thomas goes to France a second time.

1815 Thomas meets with Russian Tsar. Begins to correspond with King of Haiti.

1821 The Haitian queen and princesses stay with the Clarksons.

1833 Slavery Abolition Act is passed successfully. William Wilberforce dies.

1838 Thomas is attacked by Wilberforce's sons and many come to his defence.

1840 Thomas speaks at International Anti-Slavery Convention

1846 Thomas Clarkson dies at Playford Hall, Suffolk, 26 September.

Thinking Further Topics

1: In His Father's Footsteps

Although Thomas' father died when he was only six years old, we can see his influence in Thomas' life. Like his father, Thomas wanted to preach God's Word and was concerned by injustice. Who in your life has influenced you? Having Christian role models in our life can be a wonderful encouragement.

The apostle Paul tells the members of the Corinthian church to follow him as he follows Christ (1 Corinthians 11:1). Who do you know who follows Christ? What can you learn from the way they live?

Thomas' father helped the poor in his parish in many practical ways. He brought them food and medicine, but he also spent time explaining the gospel to them. He cared about their spiritual health as well as their physical health. In the gospels we see that Jesus did this. He fed the crowd with bread and fish and with the Word of God (Matthew 14:13-21; John 6:35). Why might it be important that we care for other people spiritually and physically? How can you show love to someone in both these ways this week?

2: A Life-changing Essay

After he finished writing his essay, Thomas was greatly troubled by the awful sufferings of the African slaves. He spent a lot of time praying, asking God what he should do. What is troubling you at the moment? Philippians 4:6 tells us we can bring anything to God in prayer. Our Father in heaven is always listening (1 Peter 3:12). Why not pray to him right now?

Thomas knew that stopping the slave trade was an impossible job for one person. Yet when he felt God calling him to do something about it in the woods, he chose to trust God. Sometimes doing the right thing feels impossible, but the Bible tells us that nothing is impossible for God (Luke 1:37). Is there an area in your life where God is calling you to trust him?

Thomas also chose to work with other Christians who were interested in abolition. God likes it when his children serve him together (Ephesians 4:1-6). Who can you ask for help when you are faced with something which seems impossible?

3: William Wilberforce

Thomas and the Abolition Society wanted to ask William Wilberforce to join them because he had a talent for public speaking and a position in Parliament. God has given us all different talents and different ways in which we can love others (Matthew 25:14-30). What talents has God given you? How might you use them to serve him?

Thomas was afraid to ask William Wilberforce to join the fight against slavery. He was so afraid he might refuse that the first time he went away without asking! If you could have spoken to Thomas before he went to visit William WIlberforce, what might you have said to encourage him? What promises does God give us when we are afraid? (See 2 Peter 1:3, Romans 8:28 and Deuteronomy 31:6 for some ideas!)

4: Danger at Liverpool!

On his travels Thomas met many people who were afraid to speak out against slavery because it would mean they would lose work, friends and perhaps even their lives. Sometimes doing the right thing can be very difficult and cost us a lot. When Jesus was on earth he said that sometimes we will suffer for following him and doing good (John 15:20-21). Have you ever experienced this?

Thomas was always very encouraged when he met those who supported abolition, such as Dr. Falconbridge. Can you think of a situation in which you might encourage other people by doing the right thing, even when it's difficult?

At Manchester, Thomas told the church that Christians are called to show mercy to others because God has shown us mercy (Luke 6:36). Jesus told his followers to love because he loved them first (John 15:12). What other reasons might you have for doing good? Why are the Bible's reasons the best ones? (1 Peter 4:11)

5: Let the People be Heard

Thomas and the abolitionists spread the truth about slavery in many creative ways: books, pamphlets,

Thomas' samples, even a carving of a chained African for jewellery! In the same way we can be creative in the ways we serve God (1 Peter 4:10). Josiah Wedgwood may not have been as talented at writing essays as Thomas was, but he did not let that stop him! Instead he produced the carving in his factory, and as a result many people stopped to consider the injustice of slavery for the first time. In what creative ways might you spread the love of Jesus this week?

The opponents of abolition made fun of the abolitionists because their witnesses were often common sailors and other poor men in lowly positions. The Bible tells us that God listens and cares about the great and the poor alike (Romans 2:11). When Jesus told the parable of the Good Samaritan, he made the despised man the hero of the story! (Luke 10:25-37) Who are you embarrassed to call your friend? How can you show them Jesus' love today?

6: Running out of Time

Thomas' journey across southern England felt like a failure. After two months of traveling, and memorising 145 questions to interview witnesses, he only managed to find nine! When have you worked hard at something, only to feel like you have failed? Thomas found comfort in the truth that although God calls us to do our best, the outcome of our work is in God's hands (Colossians 3:23; Proverbs 16:9). In times of disappointment how can you remind yourself of this?

Thomas often felt very upset when he heard about the sufferings of the Africans. The Bible tells us several times that Jesus wept while he was on earth (Luke 19:41; John 11:35). Why is it okay to feel sad when we hear about sad situations? What makes you upset? Thomas did two things with his sadness: he prayed to God, and he did his best to fight slavery. What might you be able to do next time something makes you sad?

7: Adventures in France

Thomas decided not to disguise himself before traveling to France, because he did not want to deceive anyone. In the Bible the apostle Paul works hard to share the gospel in clear and plain ways, without lying or tricking (2 Corinthians 4:2). It is not wrong to want to fit in, but as Christians it is important to remember that we represent Jesus. What are some wrong reasons for changing ourselves? What are some right ones? (1 Corinthians 9:22)

God kept Thomas safe in France. It is always wonderful when God protects his people (see Daniel 3!). Yet the Bible doesn't promise that we will not suffer (John 16:33). What it does promise is that God will never leave us, and everything will work for our good (Matthew 28:20; Romans 8:28). How can this be a comfort to you?

8: Sugar, Rum and Dangerous Waters

Many people in England decided not to eat sugar or drink rum because it was produced by slaves. Today many people choose not to buy clothes made by slaves in Third World countries or buy food from companies that treat their workers badly. It can be difficult to know how best to love our neighbours all over the world. Being aware of others' suffering is important (Hebrews 13:3). How can you find out more today?

Thomas became very ill and needed time to rest and recover. When we are sick it can be difficult to trust God. We may be angry, afraid or impatient. Yet the Bible tells us that God does not leave us when we are sick (Romans 8:38). Sick people can still love God and love their neighbour – which is what God calls us to do (Mark 12:30-31). William Cowper struggled with ill health throughout his life, yet God used his poetry to aid the abolition movement.

9: A Good Man's Happiness

It took twenty-two years after Thomas surrendered to God in the woods for the slave trade to be abolished. That's a long time! He and his fellow workers faced many discouragements. Despite these, they persevered because they knew they were doing the work of God. Sometimes following Jesus and living as a Christian can be difficult. We can experience many disappointments. How might we find the strength to persevere? (Philippians 1:6; Galatians 6:9; Romans 5:3-5)

After abolition finally succeeded, Thomas was filled with joy and praised God. It is important to remember to thank and praise God when he blesses our work.

The Bible is full of praises (Psalm 9:1; Isaiah 25:1; Acts 2:46-47)! Can you think of a time when God has worked through you? Did you thank him for it? If not, do so now!

10: The Fight Continues

Even though Thomas wanted to go to the European Congress in Vienna, he chose not to because Wilberforce did not think it wise. The Bible tells us that even though we have immense freedom as Christians, we are called to love others in all we do (Romans 14:19-20). Sometimes that might look like submitting to their advice, even when we don't agree! (Ephesians 5:21) Have you ever been in a situation like this? What did you do?

Thomas and Catherine enjoyed spending time with the Queen and princesses of Haiti. They believed that everyone is equal in God's sight, and they willingly practised what they believed by offering hospitality. The Bible tells us it is not enough to say we love Jesus, we need to live it out (James 1:22). Do you find this difficult? Remember we have God's Spirit to help us! (Galatians 5:5)

11: Come, Come, my Beloved!

When Wilberforce's sons spread lies and false accusations against Thomas, he did not do the same back. Instead he made the truth known and offered them generous forgiveness. It is so difficult to be kind to people who are not kind to us. Yet Jesus loved us while we were still his enemies! (Matthew 5:44; Romans 5:8) Who do you find difficult to love? How can you show them kindness next time you see them?

Many people praised Thomas for his abolition work. Thomas always reminded them that he could have done nothing without God and other people. He knew that as Christians we all work together for God's kingdom – just as different parts of a body work together (1 Corinthians 12:27). At the very end of his life Thomas could do nothing – but God was still working and he brought Thomas safely Home. Do you trust that God will do the same for you (John 14:2-3)?

Thomas Clarkson
(1760-1846) Life Summary

Thomas Clarkson was born in 1760 in Wisbech. His father John was a schoolteacher and clergyman with a heart for the poor and downtrodden. He died when Thomas Clarkson was only six years old, leaving behind his wife and three children. At fifteen years old Thomas was sent to London to attend school. He studied conscientiously and entered Cambridge University in 1779 after winning several prizes. He was set on following in his father's footsteps and entering the church.

Clarkson graduated from his bachelors with a first in Mathematics and became ordained as a deacon that same year. While preparing to begin his Master of Arts degree, Clarkson entered a Latin competition which would change the course of his life, and the lives of thousands of others. While researching the answer to the essay question '*Is it lawful to make slaves of others against their will?*' he became convinced that slavery was wrong and God was calling him to fight against it.

Clarkson felt inadequate to the task, and knew that opposing slavery would mean giving up a comfortable career. He met other individuals, many of whom were Quakers, who also wished to see the end of the slave trade. Eventually he could stall no longer, and committed his entire life to the abolition of slavery.

After the publication of his essay, Clarkson and his like-minded friends established the *Society for the Abolition of the Slave Trade*. Thomas' main task was collecting evidence to prove the evils of slavery. He worked night and day, making long, perilous journeys across land and sea to find witnesses unafraid to testify against the horrific treatment of slaves and sailors. Once he was almost thrown into the ocean by those who opposed abolition. He assembled beautiful specimens of African art to show alongside the torture equipment used on the slave ships, storing them both in what would come to be known as 'Clarkson's Box'.

Clarkson also spoke with both William Wilberforce and William Pitt, showing them the evidence he had collected against the slave trade. They agreed to join him and the Society to bring the matter before Parliament year after year. While they did so, Thomas continued to work behind the scenes, collecting evidence, petitions, and even visiting France to encourage the abolitionists there.

After working hard for many years, Clarkson was forced by ill health to rest from his tiring journeys and demanding schedule. He married, moved to the Lake District, and turned to farming, befriending several poets who lived nearby. One of them, Coleridge, called him a 'moral steam-engine' and the 'giant with one idea'. This proved true, because even during this period Thomas didn't stop campaigning for justice, helping the poor in the village and even going door-knocking for missing cows!

When the slave trade was abolished in 1807, Clarkson didn't slow down. He began working towards abolition of slavery itself, writing copious books, pamphlets and letters. Clarkson believed strongly that people should have the evidence to make informed decisions, and so he also wrote three volumes on the Quakers, an often misunderstood religious minority, as well as several works on aspects of Christianity.

In 1833 slavery officially became illegal in the British Isles. At last Thomas' country agreed with the essay he had written all those years ago: It is *never* lawful to make slaves of others against their will.

Half-blind and struggling with arthritis, Clarkson received a standing ovation from 5,000 delegates from nine different countries at the Anti-Slavery Convention in 1840. He charged them to 'take courage, do not be dismayed, go on, persevere to the last,' because the task ahead of them was the removal of slavery from the 'whole world.'

In 1846, Thomas Clarkson died and went to be with his beloved Saviour. He refused a tombstone and was buried in a simple ceremony with a eulogy from one of his many Quaker friends.

Modern Day Slavery

Although African Slavery was abolished in Britain in 1833, slavery still exists in many forms today. In some countries poor parents are forced to sell their children or themselves into slavery in order to buy food or pay off a debt. In other countries, young women are promised safe passage and a new life in another place, only to find themselves held captive and forced to do terrible jobs. Companies which refuse to pay their workers fair wages or give them good working conditions also practise slavery. It is estimated that in 2020 there are over 40 million slaves all over the world, and one in four are children!

The fight against slavery is not over, but take heart. We are not fighting this great evil in our own strength, but are joining in the work of our Saviour, who came to 'proclaim freedom for the prisoners' and 'to set the oppressed free.' (Luke 4:18)

For more stories of modern day slavery, see: https://www.ijm.org/slavery

For a list of organisations working to combat slavery and what you can do to help, see: http://www.endslaverynow.org/connect

About the Author

Emily J. Maurits devoured Trail Blazer books as a child, and is thrilled to introduce the latest generation of readers to Thomas Clarkson. His story is a reminder that dedicating our lives to doing one thing well can be a courageous act of faith. This is what Thomas Clarkson did – and God used him to change the world! Following Jesus will never be boring if, like Thomas, we are willing to listen to God's voice and step out in trust. Emily writes about loving family and friends with chronic illnesses at www.calledtowatch.com and hopes that the story of Thomas Clarkson will inspire many to tread with perseverance the path God has called them to walk.

OTHER BOOKS IN THE TRAIL BLAZERS SERIES

For a full list of Trail Blazers, please see our
website: www.christianfocus.com
All Trail Blazers are available as e-books

Francis & Edith Schaeffer
Taking on the World
by Rachel Lane

Two young people, one faith and a shared passion for the truth of God's Word – that was the beginning of the story of Francis and Edith Schaeffer. Together, they wanted to follow wherever God would lead them and to share the Good News about Jesus with whoever God would send them. But little did they imagine that God would lead them to a remote village in the mountains of Switzerland. Nor did they foresee how God would use their ministry in that little mountain chalet to impact people all over the world.

Francis and Edith Schaeffer opened their home to anyone searching for truth. They spent their whole lives helping people to see that the Bible's answers to life's questions are relevant and true; in their time, and for all time.

ISBN: 978-1-5271-0300-9

Elizabeth Prentiss
More Love
by Claire Williams

Elizabeth was a bright young girl who knew what it was
to have a heart sore with troubles. Born in Portland,
Maine in the United States, Elizabeth was deeply
impacted by the death of her father, who suffered from
tuberculosis. However, in those early days she found
that Jesus Christ and his love was her strength.

Living life as a Christian wife and mother didn't
mean that suffering became part of her past. She also
had health problems and two of her own children died.

Elizabeth Prentiss continued to turn to her loving
Heavenly Father for love and support, while also using
her talent with the pen to bring glory to God and help
to others in their time of need.

ISBN: 978-1-5271-0299-6

John Chrysostom
The Preacher in the Emperor's Court
by Dayspring MacLeod

There was something about John Chrysostom and the words he spoke that lit up his world.

He was an important leader of the early church, known so much for his preaching and public speaking that he was given the nickname Golden Mouth. He spoke his mind and followed his convictions.

It didn't matter if you were rich or poor John spoke the truth – emphatically. Even the empress fell under his criticism which eventually led to his exile and death.

ISBN: 978-1-5271-0308-5

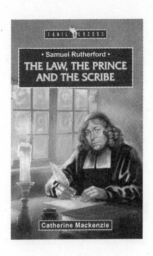

Samuel Rutherford

The Law, the Prince and the Scribe
by Catherine MacKenzie

When Samuel Rutherford picked up his pen he changed lives. His book Lex Rex was burned on a pyre but his notes of comfort and wisdom were cherished by those he cared to guide and counsel. Accused of treason he died of illness before there was time to make him a martyr and on his gravestone today, just west of the Bell Tower in St. Andrews Cathedral are engraved the striking words that sum up his life, 'Acquainted with Emmanuel's Love'.

ISBN: 978-1-5271-0309-2

John and Betty Stam
To Die is Gain
by Rachel Lane

John and Betty Stam were a young missionary couple sent to China in the 1930s. It was a dangerous time and place to stand for Christ, but John and Betty knew the risks. All they wanted was to spend their lives sharing the good news of Jesus with those who had never heard it. This is a story of tragedy as well as trust. It is a story of great sacrifice, as well as hope. It is the story of two young martyrs who were willing to pay the ultimate price in their service of Christ.

ISBN: 978-1-5271-0530-0

Maud Kells

Fearless in the Forest

by Jean Gibson

At 25 years of age Maud Kells went to the Congo as a
medical missionary with WEC International. She went
to replace others who had been recently martyred.
Years later she herself found herself close to death on
the floor of her own operating theatre. A rebel soldier's
bullet went straight through her and only the Lords
grace and her presence of mind saved her life in the
end. This is the story of a young Irish girl who went to
Africa despite her family's objections due to the crystal
clear call on her life of a God who assured her, 'I am
with you I am all you need'. Maud found that out to
be absolutely true in all circumstances.

ISBN: 978-1-5271-0529-4

CHRISTIAN FOCUS PUBLICATIONS

Christian Focus | Christian Heritage | CF4K | Mentor

Christian Focus Publications publishes books for adults and children under its four main imprints: Christian Focus, CF4K, Mentor and Christian Heritage. Our books reflect our conviction that God's Word is reliable and Jesus is the way to know him, and live for ever with him.

Our children's publication list includes a Sunday School curriculum that covers pre-school to early teens, and puzzle and activity books. We also publish personal and family devotional titles, biographies and inspirational stories that children will love.

If you are looking for quality Bible teaching for children then we have an excellent range of Bible stories and age-specific theological books.

From pre-school board books to teenage apologetics, we have it covered!

Find us at our web page:
www.christianfocus.com

CF4•K
Because you're never
too young to know Jesus